A European Sojourn
1943-1945

AN AUTOBIOGRAPHY

PVT. FREDERICK O. SCHEER
SERIAL NO. 14118781

AS RECOUNTED TO
REAR ADMIRAL WILLIAM O. MILLER
J A G C USN (RET.)

Printed in the United States of America.

ISBN: 978-1-4269-6335-3

Library of Congress Control Number: 2011910664

Trafford rev. 09/08/2011

 www.trafford.com

North America & international
toll-free: 1 888 232 4444 (USA & Canada)
phone: 250 383 6864 ♦ fax: 812 355 4082

A European Sojourn
1943-1945
An Autobiography

Pvt. Frederick O. Scheer
Serial No. 14118781

As recounted to
Rear Admiral William O. Miller
J A G C USN (Ret.)

Pvt. Frederick O. Scheer, 14118781

In loving memory of Florence and George Scheer, Sr.

Acknowledgments

Several people helped me with the production of this book. First, I must say something about my good friend Rear Admiral William O. Miller, J A G C USN (Ret.), known to me and all his friends as Dusty. What a guy! One morning while drinking coffee before our Kiwanis meeting, I started recounting with Dusty and a few others some of the funny experiences I had had as a POW in World War II. Dusty commented that I should write it all down so my grandchildren would have it. That sounded like a good idea and, knowing he had a flair for writing, I asked him if he would help me. That led to many, many hours together and this book is the result. I want to say how amazing Dusty is and how much I thank him for all he did to make this book happen.

Thanks also go to Marcia Rothschild, M.Ed., who edited the copy, advised me concerning structure and style, and assisted with formatting and layout.

Throughout the book are copies of Western Union Telegrams, photographs, newspaper clippings, military orders and other items I had either mailed or brought home, or that were collected by my beloved older sister, Gloria. Now, after more than sixty years, these objects are preserved in a scrapbook she made for me, except for one that has long since disintegrated—a German chocolate bar.

To acknowledge the help, support and encouragement that I received from my wonderful wife, Gerry is hardly enough. She made it possible for me to complete this story of my World War II adventure.

Frederick O. Scheer

TABLE OF CONTENTS

CHAPTER ONE
Beginning an Uncertain Adventure

Early on a beautiful Georgia spring day, April 6, 1943, less than 18 months after the Japanese bombed Pearl Harbor, a young farm boy from Eatonton, Georgia, marched tremulously through the main gate of Fort McPherson to report pursuant to orders from the United States Army. I was that young man.

At this point I knew all too well the meaning of the expression "fear of the unknown." I had been in places with lots of people, but nothing like this. It seemed as though there were thousands and thousands of guys. And then there were these big barracks-type buildings that looked like two-story barns. They were all over the place and seemed to go on forever.

It was quite a revelation to witness the machinations of the induction center at Fort McPherson. I had spent the previous year as a member of the cavalry ROTC at the University of Georgia, but the real Army was clearly something else! And there were no horses.

My first week of active duty as an Army enlisted reservist was consumed with the normal checking-in processes. One poignant memory was the all-encompassing importance of the Private First Class who was the incoming clerk at the reception center. This fellow held my entire future in his hands, as well as those of several thousand other new American soldiers from throughout the Southeast. He didn't just handle papers; he was assigned a group of us, and he herded his little flock from place to place.

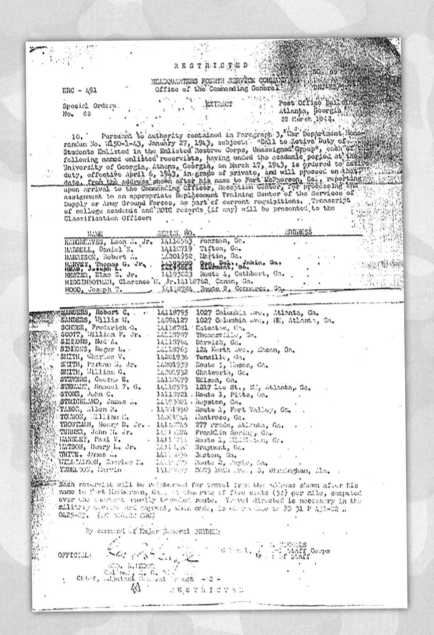

RESTRICTED

HEADQUARTERS FOURTH SERVICE COMMAND
Office of the Commanding General

ERC - 491

Special Orders   EXTRACT   Post Office Building
No. 69   Atlanta, Georgia
                                          22 March 1944

10.   Pursuant to authority contained in Paragraph 3, War Department Memorandum No. W150-1-43, January 27, 1943, subject: "Call to Active Duty of Students Enlisted in the Enlisted Reserve Corps, Unassigned Group", each of following named enlisted reservists, having ended the academic period at the University of Georgia, Athens, Georgia, on March 17, 1943, is ordered to active duty, effective April 6, 1943, in grade of private, and will proceed on that date from the address shown after his name to Fort McPherson, Ga., reporting upon arrival to the Commanding Officer, Reception Center, for processing and assignment to an appropriate Replacement Training Center of the Services of Supply or Army Ground Forces, as part of current requisitions. Transcript of college academic and ROTC records (if any) will be presented to the Classification Officer:

NAME	SERIAL NO.	ADDRESS
HARGREAVES, Leon A. Jr.	14118563	Pearson, Ga.
HARRELL, Daniel N.	14118719	Tifton, Ga.
HARRISON, Robert A.	14201952	Martin, Ga.
HARVEY, Thomas G. Jr.	14293020	Gen. Del., Jakin, Ga.
HEAD, Joseph E.	14193021	Piedmont, Ga.
HESTER, Elmo C. Jr.	14193023	Route 4, Cuthbert, Ga.
HIGGINBOTHAM, Clarence R. Jr.	14118762	Canon, Ga.
HOOD, Joseph T.	14118784	Route 2, Commerce, Ga.

SANDERS, Robert C.	14118795	1027 Columbia Ave., Atlanta, Ga.
SANDERS, Willis W.	14094127	1027 Columbia Ave., SE, Atlanta, Ga.
SCHER, Frederick G.	14118781	Eatonton, Ga.
SCOTT, William F. Jr.	14118787	Thomasville, Ga.
SHEDDS, Ned A.	14118764	Berwick, Ga.
SIMMONS, Roger L.	14118765	124 North Ave., Macon, Ga.
SMITH, Charles V.	14201936	Tennille, Ga.
SMITH, Parham W. Jr.	14201939	Route 5, Macon, Ga.
SMITH, William G.	14201932	Chatworth, Ga.
STEVENS, George E.	14118579	Edison, Ga.
STEWART, Samuel F. G.	14118575	1217 Lee St., SW, Atlanta, Ga.
STONE, John C.	14118721	Route 1, Pitts, Ga.
STRICKLAND, James A.	14193021	Royston, Ga.
TABOR, Allen R.	14201950	Route 3, Fort Valley, Ga.
TOWSON, William R.	14201941	Montrose, Ga.
TROUTMAN, Henry D. Jr.	14118745	277 Prado, Atlanta, Ga.
TURNER, John W. Jr.	14118744	Franklin Spring, Ga.
WANSLEY, Paul V.	14118755	Route 1, Middleton, Ga.
WATSON, Henry L. Jr.	14118751	Graymont, Ga.
WHITE, James A.	14118456	Buston, Ga.
WILLIAMSON, Charles R.	14118757	Route 2, Doyle, Ga.
YUDELSON, Marvin	14118767	3409 10th Ave., S, Birmingham, Ala.

Each reservist will be reimbursed for travel from the address shown after his name to Fort McPherson, Ga., at the rate of five cents (5¢) per mile, computed over the shortest usually traveled route. Travel directed is necessary in the military service and payment, when made, is chargeable to FD 31 P 431-02 A 0425-22. (A2 ROBAE, ERC)

By command of Major General BRYDEN:

OFFICIAL: NICHOLS
                                       Colonel, General Staff Corps
GEO. A. KELSO,   Chief of Staff
Colonel, A. G. D.,
Chief, Adjutant General Branch   -2-

RESTRICTED

These are my orders to report for active duty.

2

This was also my introduction to a new approach to making friends. I would quickly get to know and like one or another of the new GIs. We would become fast friends, but the friendships would last only as long as we were stationed together. The first of these friendships lasted only the two weeks until we were shipped out, but was memorable nonetheless. We were just hanging around one afternoon, when one of the guys and I decided to smoke a cigar. We vowed then and there to smoke cigars whenever we met in the future. I never saw that guy again. The two weeks at Ft. Mac with our fearless leader, the PFC, were hectic, filled with the minutiae required to get us inducted and ready for the trip to our next destination—which we had not yet been told was to be Fort Riley, Kansas. As we prepared ourselves for departure, I called home to tell my parents good-bye, but I couldn't tell them where I was going. That was a military secret and this pack of new recruits was definitely going to be the last to know. The whole experience was becoming a real adventure for me. Eatonton, Georgia was nothing like this.

Our journey began at the end of the second week of April 1943, when a troop train backed into Fort McPherson and thousands of new soldiers climbed aboard, including one Frederick O. Scheer, who was making only his second venture outside the state of Georgia. The trip took about five days. We traveled through some strange places that I had never heard of before—like Evansville, Indiana. And there were these wide open expanses of land that must have been great to farm. I thought about how much I'd like to crank up that old green John Deere tractor and tiller of ours and head out across one of those fields. You could just go on forever before you had to turn around. When we arrived at Fort Riley, we were on the arid plains of Kansas. And they were arid, indeed!!

The farm boy: Frederick, age 4.

IDENTIFICATION CARD— ENLISTED RESERVE CORPS

This is to Certify, That **Frederick Oscar Scheer, Pvt., Unasgd.**
Serial No. **14,118,781** Home Address **Eatonton, Georgia**
was {transferred to / enlisted in} *grade shown in **PRIVATE**
Enlisted Reserve Corps of the Army of the United States, on the **10th** day of
December, one thousand nine hundred and **forty-two**, for
the period of **Duration of War plus six (6) months**. When enlisted *he was **18** years of age, and
by occupation a **STUDENT**. He has **Hazel** eyes, **Black**
hair, **Ruddy** complexion, and is **5** feet **9** inches in height.
Dates of immunization: Smallpox _____ Typhoid _____
_____ Other _____ **3** Blood type
_____

Given at Headquarters **ROTC, Univ of Ga., Athens, Ga.**, this
10th day of **December** one thousand nine hundred and **forty-two**.
* Cross out words not applicable.
FOR THE COMMANDING OFFICER _____
W. D., A. G. O. Form No. 166—March
KERR P. RIGGS
Col Gov

I received this ID card when I volunteered for the enlisted reserves while at the University of Georgia in December 1942.

4

CHAPTER TWO
Down and Dirty - Basic Training
Fort Riley, Kansas

The first thing we had to do was move into one of the tar-paper huts that abounded at Fort Riley. Most of these buildings were used as living quarters for the trainees; a few served as command offices and one as the mess hall. There was one large theater building and the all-important PX. This collection of structures was to be our home during our 13 weeks of infantry training.

The tar-paper barracks were something out of the dark ages. They were long and narrow, with one row of cots on either side. Each bed had a foot locker in front of it and a shelf above it on the wall. The barracks were heated by three large pot-bellied stoves stationed along the full length of the center aisle. I don't think I knew a single member of this new company when we arrived, but it wasn't long before we all knew everyone in the barracks.

The wind blew steadily across the Republican Flats, as this area along the Republican River was known, and it stirred up mounds and mounds of dust that readily penetrated the walls of our barracks. The sergeant gave us brooms and told us to sweep the hut, which we did . . . and did . . . and did. By the time we had swept the full length of the hut, we had to start all over again because the dust was coming in faster than we could sweep it out. By the third or fourth trip down the middle of the barracks, we learned the meaning of "what the hell" and quit.

We were each issued an M-1 rifle, straight out of the box, still covered with Cosmoline, a type of petroleum jelly very much like Vaseline. This jelly protected the rifles until they were put into service. I remember removing my Cosmoline-covered rifle from the packing case. We could actually see the dust floating in the air in the hut, and this caused great consternation as we tried to clean our new rifles. It seems that dust, when mixed with Cosmoline, creates a wonderfully gritty compound suitable for use in grinding—an effect it undoubtedly had on our new guns.

These rifles, though, were really something special. I'll admit I was no gun expert; other than a pump BB gun, I had never owned a weapon of any kind. This new rifle weighed about nine pounds and had a clip that held eight rounds of ammunition. It was semi-automatic, which meant you could pull the trigger repeatedly and the gun would fire a round with each pull. After eight rounds had been fired, the clip would pop out automatically, allowing you to pop in a full clip and continue firing.

As it happened, our hut was located next door to the mess hall, whose most famous resident was the sergeant in charge of the hall. This particular sergeant, our mess sergeant, liked his beer and had the beer belly to prove it. He would spend almost every evening after chow partaking of his favorite pleasure to the point that, when he returned to the hut at about 2100 hours (9 PM) in a distinctly inebriated condition, he would attack the pot-bellied stoves, banging into each one in turn as he stumbled his way down the center of the hut. Frequently the stove would win, ensnaring the sergeant in its smoke stack and covering him with soot. It seems amazing that this behavior was allowed to continue, but it was, and the mess sergeant continued to oversee the preparation of our food throughout our thirteen weeks at Fort Riley.

The mess sergeant and his cooks were not the only ones to see the inside of the mess hall at times other than mess time. There is a duty known to all GI's as KP. Often this duty is used as punishment for breaking the rules, and the sergeant could always find as many rule-breakers as he needed for kitchen duty. This duty could involve scrubbing the floors or washing the tremendous pots and pans, but the job we feared the most was peeling potatoes. Have you ever seen a mountain of potatoes? Or maybe I should say a nightmare of potatoes? You would peel and peel and peel, and the pile would seem to grow bigger and bigger and bigger. Potato day was endless. And we didn't have any of those neat little potato-peeler gadgets. We used knives—and I'll bet we peeled off tons of good potato along with the skins, but we didn't even care.

Everyone who lived through this period remembers the Andrews Sisters and their "Boogie Woogie Bugle Boy." As it turned out, sleeping on the cot next to mine in our beautiful tar-paper hut was a young man of Greek ancestry from Albany, Georgia who was an accomplished trumpet player. Because of that skill, he became the renowned "Bugle Boy of Company B" and I, somewhat unavoidably, became the "pup that woke the bugler up."

It wasn't dusty and windy all the time at Fort Riley. On some occasions the rain would come down in torrents, so much so that the ground would become soggy. The Fort Riley soil was of some special variety that, when mixed with water, became a clinging, sucking

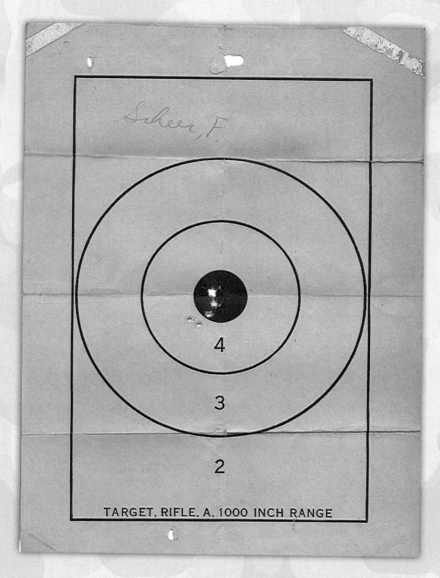

Scheer, F.

4

3

2

TARGET, RIFLE, A, 1000 INCH RANGE

Not bad shooting, Pvt. Scheer!!

muck. An infantryman slogging through it could easily lose his boots—in fact, I did lose mine once.

Although Fort Riley was a cavalry center, at the beginning of 1943 it was also being used as a training center for infantry replacements. In these early days of World War II, the cavalry still had horses. Most of the cavalry was mechanized—tanks, armored personnel carriers and the like—but believe it or not, the officers at Fort Riley still rode horses around the fort and always rode them for retreat.

The training we received was essentially divided into three categories. The first was close-order drill, the goal of which was to instill in the soldier the required discipline along with the rigid understanding that when an order is given by a superior, it was to be followed correctly and promptly. Our platoon sergeant made this latter point abundantly clear. He admonished us to "Obey, Obey, Obey, Obey, any order from a superior, promptly and without question." When a young, squeaky Yankee voice from the back row queried, "You mean, if someone tells me to go out in that field and bring back a pile of shit and I don't want to go out there and get that pile of stinking shit, I have to do it anyway?", the sergeant gruffly replied, "You bet your sweet ass you better bring back that pile of shit—and do it damn quick."

The second element was physical training that had as its objective to bring the young soldier into a physical condition such that he could endure the physical stress of battle. The most memorable parts of this were calisthenics—rain or shine—and the 25-mile hikes with a full field pack that weighed about 50 pounds. This took a great deal of stamina.

One morning we were marched out to a large flat (flat being not unusual in Kansas) area facing a dirt embankment for our morning calisthenics. The sergeant climbed to the top of the barrier and blew his whistle to start the exercising. Just as we got into full swing doing jumping jacks (the exercise where you jump, spreading your legs while flinging your arms over your head), it started to rain. Now this was no ordinary rain: The drops were as big as quarters. Every time my arms went up, my raincoat filled with water. After about 20 minutes of this, the rain growing even harder, an officer rode up to the top of the dike at a fast gallop and shouted at the sergeant to, "Get these men back to the barracks!" Boy, were we glad to get out of that mess!

The third element was technical training, which taught the soldier how to meld himself into a unit of other soldiers, how to handle his weapon properly and repair it properly if need be, and how to use that weapon in a battlefield environment in coordination and conjunction with his fellow soldiers. An absolutely essential requirement was the ability to disassemble and reassemble an M-1 rifle—blindfolded. This activity involved going to the rifle range where we were divided into two groups. One group was stationed along a firing line; the other was sent to the pits below the targets. Each time the guys on the firing line would try their luck at hitting the target, the guys in the pits would hold long poles with large black disks at the end to show a spotter where the shooter had hit the target (if he had). Working in the pits was both good and bad. The good was that you were in a place where the sergeant could not see you; the bad was the amount of work involved, not to mention the bullets flying over your head and an occasional ricochet.

Another part of technical training was the obstacle course. This came in two parts. First we had to run a track that was filled with obstacles to maneuver over, under, around, across and through. These included 10-foot walls, strings of car tires lying on the ground, large pipes representing tunnels, overhead bars, and on and on and on. But the real test was to keep from getting your butt shot off. In one exercise you had to crawl across an open area on your belly with your rifle cradled in your arms—with machine-gun fire crisscrossing just above your head and the sergeant shouting, "Keep your head down, Stupid!" Just to add a little excitement, from time to time an explosion would go off somewhere nearby. Surprisingly, no one was ever hurt.

Often the company would assemble, en mass, in the theater to see a movie. Before the film started, an officer would go up on the stage in front of us and demand to know if we all had handkerchiefs, and if so, he wanted to see them. Can you imagine all these people holding their handkerchiefs above their heads and waving them so the officer could see them—and, of course, spreading germs all over the place? Then on one occasion the officer was a medic. He had a fit when he saw all those handkerchiefs waving, and that was the last of that. One film we saw was entitled "Why We Fight" and was intended to pump us up and put us in a fighting mood. We were also regularly shown a sex film. Unfortunately, it was not the sort of sex film guys our age wanted to see. This movie told us all the grim things about venereal diseases and how to avoid catching one.

One day our platoon was sitting in the barracks getting a lecture on something or other when there was a shout from outside to clear the barracks. There was a tornado coming our way! We all ran out and headed for shelter in the lowest place we could find. I found a spot in a ditch and got down in it. Actually, it was just a small tornado, but it was the first I had ever seen. I heard a noise and looked up to see part of the roof of a building being dragged toward me. Fortunately it stopped before it got to me. Our barracks was not damaged, and none of us was hurt.

. . . . .

As part of our training, and to give us confidence as leaders, the sergeant would choose one of us to be in charge of the barracks on inspection day. The GI in charge of the barracks was to see that all bunks were properly made, floors clean, foot lockers neat inside and out, and the whole barracks shipshape in every way—including the barracks captain being neatly shaved and dressed for the inspection. Guess who had that wonderful chance to prove his leadership ability one beautiful morning: none other than yours truly, ol' Frederick O. himself.

That morning the barracks did look good. With a little arm twisting from me, the guys had cleaned up their act. The trouble was that I was so busy seeing that everyone else did what they should do that I did not get into the latrine to shave. I thought, "Well I'll just wing it." I did, but it didn't. When the command came to fall out, all of our guys rushed out of the barracks smartly. I, as barracks captain, did not have to fall out for assembly. I waited in the barracks for the officer to come by to make the inspection. When our turn came—and it came first—the sergeant and captain strode up to the door of the barracks and I very smartly shouted at the top of my lungs "ATTENTION." (Of course, I was the only one to come to attention, as I was the only private there.)

The inspection went well. The captain and sergeant did their usual things, like checking to see if foot lockers were neat and the barracks in general was neat and clean. They even checked to see if the bunks were made up tight and handsome. I personally thought the inspection went off great. That was, until the captain as he was leaving said to me, "Soldier, did you shave this morning?" Under the circumstances of course, I lied and said "YES SIR." Well, believe it or not, officers are not that dumb. We got a gig and extra duty for my not shaving. Needless to say, there were a few comments around the barracks about that.

Remember that squeaky Yankee kid I mentioned earlier? Well, one morning the company officers were holding a session in the barracks to allow us to air complaints. This guy, again in the back of the room, raised his hand and when recognized, stood up and said, " Why is it that when we don't have enough hot water in the morning to shave, the officers come in and just let the hot water run while they shave and then tell us to conserve water?" He was a bit brazen or, we thought, just Yankee, but it worked. The officers no longer let the water run while they shaved.

And shepherding all of us through the entire basic training experience at Fort Riley was our tough buck sergeant who, just like the ones you see in the movies, would get right in your face and shout and shout and shout!

CHAPTER THREE
In Transit

Thirteen weeks after arriving at Fort Riley, we again boarded a troop train, this time headed for Camp Butner, North Carolina. Hot and sweaty Camp Butner was just a short sojourn between Fort Riley and Fort George Meade, Maryland, but it did provide a seven-day furlough for us to go home and visit family and friends. Within a couple of weeks I was given a seven-day pass to go home and called my parents to tell them when my train would arrive in Atlanta.

Oh, what a memorable train ride it was! I met a lovely southern belle who seemed to be taken with me. Being a big spender, I asked if she would like a coke. She drawled, "Of course. That would be nice." So off I went in search of some Coca-Colas and soon found myself wandering toward the back of the train. My search ended when, entering one car, I was shocked to see that it was entirely occupied by Negroes—soldiers and civilians alike—except for the conductor, who was white. Seeing me, he said, "Son, you are not supposed to be in this car. Go back up front in the white people's car." When I told him I was just looking for some Cokes, he told me again, this time with special emphasis, "You ain't supposed to be here. Go back up front where you belong." At that point, I complied. He did, however, agree to sell me six, hot, nickel Cokes for a quarter apiece.

One might think that, being a southerner, one who was raised with colored people in a small southern town, I should have been aware of what segregation looked like. I suppose on some level I was, but this was a shock to me—a graphic example of what segregation in the South was all about. And I didn't like it.

In addition, it seems I had neglected to tell my parents at which of Atlanta's two railroad stations I was scheduled to arrive. Maybe I had forgotten to say, or maybe I just didn't know, but the omission caused a significant problem for Mother and Dad. Believe you me, they let me hear about how they had run the two long blocks from one station to the other as trains arrived at both stations at about the same time. Their distress was soon overshadowed, though, by their pleasure at having their little boy home again, if only for a few days.

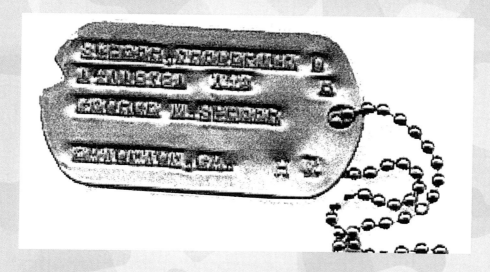

SCHEER, FREDERICK O
14118781   T45   B
GEORGE M. SCHEER
EATONTON, GA.   H ꟷ

This is my corrected dog tag.

Still the farm boy, I wanted to see what had been going on while I had been away, so Mother and Daddy and I went out to our two family farms to see my favorite purebred Guernsey heifers. I also wanted to see Hick and Buster, two of our Black farm hands with whom I had worked for years and on whom our family depended. Hick and Buster were not only farm help. They were friends.

I remember that my parents and I were riding to the farms and they were asking about my experiences while away, I injected the word "hell" into my comments rather frequently. I would say, "And hell, we would do this," or "And hell, we would do that." Dad stood it as long as he could, but finally interrupted me saying "Hell this, hell that hell, hell." With that I dropped the "helling" and talked normally.

The couple of weeks at Camp Butner before getting the pass home had been spent in training. This training primarily involved crawling through underbrush and poison ivy. Guess what? By the time my pass came through I had one hell of a case of poison ivy. It was in my eyes, on my face, down my arms—just about all over my body. It was so bad that I went out to Ft. McPherson for treatment. The doctor there tied to tell me I had athlete's foot in my eyes, the result of rubbing my toes and then rubbing my eyes. He was finally persuaded that it was poison ivy and gave me a shot that cured me in a few days.

Also while at Camp Butner, I had noticed that my dog tags had P stamped on them, indicating that my religious preference was Protestant. I decided to have this changed to an H for Hebrew. I told some of the guys in the barracks what I intended to do. I can still hear one of my friends saying, "You mean you are going to ask that anti-Semitic SOB sergeant to change your dog tags?" I went ahead and asked. He didn't give me any grief, but little did I suspect the problems this change might cause me later.

After returning from furlough and receiving some additional training, we shipped out to Ft. George Mead, Maryland. Upon arrival each of us was issued a full set of field equipment. This included new uniforms, a field pack, a rifle, a bayonet and all the other equipment we would need when we joined the unit to which we would be assigned. Each soldier in our group was designated as an "Individual Infantry Replacement." No one had yet been assigned to any unit.

When we had received our equipment my group shipped out to the European Theater of Operations (ETO)—everyone, that is, except me. I had been issued GI eyeglasses and I

B'NAI BRITH-FAYETTEVILLE & HARGETT STREETS

Lounge, Reading Room, Writing Facilities, Games
SATURDAY: 2-12 PM Dancing, Refreshments, Housing Assistance
SUNDAY: 4-6 PM Refreshments

TRAVELERS' AID --336½ S. Salisbury Street
Travel Information, Directions and
Referrals to Cmmunity Resources
INFORMATION BOOTH AT BUS STATION
Phone 3-1911 Appointments at Bus and
Railway Stations

RED CROSS
102 W. Hargett Street
Service to Transient
Servicemen

CHURCH CENTERS

TABERNACLE BAPTIST
Corner Hargett & Person Streets
Saturdays: 2:30-11:30 PM--Games
and Refreshments
Sunday; 2:30 to 6:00 PM
Housing Service through USO-YMCA
CALVARY BAPTIST: South and
Fayetteville Streets--Housing for
Servicemen, Games and Refreshments
Lounge, Open Saturday 3:00-12:00
Open Sunday except Church Hours
Hostess: Mrs. Alma Bell
WEST RALEIGH PRESBYTERIAN
Corner Horne Street & Vanderbilt
Avenue
Housing Service Through USO-YMCA
Sunday--Breakfast
SALVATION ARMY: 213 S. Person Street
Housing in cooperation with USO-
YMCA; USO Club, 424½ Fayetteville
Street--Open every day 9 AM to 11 PM

CHRIST EPISCOPAL
N. E. Corner Capitol Square
Saturday: 4 to 6 PM--Reading,
Writing, Housing Service in
cooperation with USO-YMCA
Sunday: Breakfast
4:00 to 8:30 Social Tea Hour
8:30--Young People's Service
Group
HAYES-BARTON BAPTIST: Five Point
6:45--Young People's Service
Group
EDENTON STREET METHODIST:
West Edenton Street--Housing
Service through USO-YMCA, Lounge,
Reading, Writing Facilities,
Sunday--Breakfast
SUNDAY: The Churches of Raleigh
and Surrounding Committees
extend a cordial invitation to
attend services. Church locaters
at USO-YMCA

LIBRARIES

North Carolina State Library
Fayetteville & Morgan Streets
Opposite Capitol
Open daily 9 AM to 5 PM
Not Open Sundays

Olivia Rainey Library
Salisbury & Hillsboro Streets
Opposite Capitol--Open Weekdays
9:30 AM to 9:00 PM & Sundays
2:00 PM to 6:00 PM

STATE CAPITOL BUILDING

Open daily from 9 AM to 5 PM

NOTICE TO ALL OFFICERS

RALEIGH OFFICERS' CLUB--ACADEMY BUILDING--BACK OF U.S. POST OFFICE
Open Saturdays and Sundays--Lounge and usual Club Facilities

NEGRO CENTERS

DAVIE STREET PRESBYTERIAN CHURCH
Davie and Person Streets (N)
Recreation Room, Lounge, Games, etc.
Supervised by Raleigh Recreation Comm.
NEGRO USO COMMITTEE HDQS.
132 E. Hargett Street
Open daily--10 AM to 6 PM
General Services--Information etc.
TUTTLE COMMUNITY CENTER
310 N. Tarboro Street
Lounge, Reading Room
RICHARD B. HARRISON PUBLIC LIBRARY
135 E. Hargett Street
Monday and Tuesday 12-9 AM
Wednesday, Thursday, and Friday
12-6 PM
Saturday--10 AM to 9 PM

DANCES FOR NEGRO TROOPS
Saturday, August 28th, 427½ S.
Blount Street (Masonic Temple)
8:30 to 11:30 in cooperation
with USO-YMCA
CHAVIS HEIGHTS CENTER
401 East Lenoir Street
Open daily 9 AM
Operated by Recreational Comm.
Lounge, Reading Room, Games,
Housing information
U.S. ARMY RECREATIONAL AREA CAMP
Take Cabarrus Street Bus
Recreation and Housing Information
Showers, Reading Room, Writing
Facilities, Games

There were many recreational and religious facilities near Camp Butner.

had not received them in time to leave with my group, so instead of just sitting around the barracks I went to the supply room to help hand out equipment. The supply sergeant liked my help, and I became a regular in the supply room for two or three weeks until my glasses arrived.

It was October, 1943, and the weather was still quite warm. I remember one evening after we had been handing out equipment for hours and there was still a whole lot more to do, the sergeant motioned me over. I had noticed that from time to time one of the other men working behind the counter would slip away quietly to the back room for a few minutes and then return to work. The sergeant motioned me to the back room, telling me there was something back there for me. I was somewhat confused, but I went anyway. What I found was a quart of beer waiting for me. Problem was, I didn't drink. I was my father's boy and he did not drink. When I saw what it was, I went back to work without touching it, but thanked the sergeant anyway. These days, though, I am sure I would not have passed up the chance to imbibe.

One weekend a couple of guys from New York who were permanent workers in the stockroom asked me if I wanted to get a pass to go into New York. I agreed and we three got passes for the weekend. I had an uncle in New York and I remembered his address, but headed out without calling him or my aunt. We took a train into the city and as we were discussing the upcoming weekend, the guys told me how to get to 118 East Eighth Street. One of them looked at me in a bit of surprise and asked, "Isn't that a Jewish neighborhood?" And I said "I really don't know, but I'm Jewish." With that the other guy said "Hell, you don't look like any Jew I ever knew, or act or sound like one, and I've lived in New York all my life." With that I said, "Hell, I don't know about that. All I know is I'm Jewish."

I'll never forget knocking on my Uncle Sam's front door, standing in the dark, and waiting and waiting, and knocking again, until someone called down from an upper window, "Who is knocking at the door at this time of night? Who is knocking?" I was a little scared. Maybe I was at the wrong house and, if so, where would I go? I answered "I am George's boy Frederick, from Eatonton." And my uncle said "Did you say you are George's son?" I said yes, and with that they came down and let me in with open arms. It was a nice weekend. Sunday afternoon my three cousins, whom I hardly knew, walked me to the subway and told me how to catch the train back to camp.

Before long my glasses came through and I was sent to the port of embarkation at Shanango, Pennsylvania. Just before departing Ft. Mead I was promoted to what we called a "salt water corporal." I immediately sewed on the two stripes. My mother would be so proud; she always wanted me to be an officer. I would be travelling with a new group of guys that I had helped equip just days earlier, and the Company Commander had written a letter of commendation for my hard work in the supply center. The letter would go on my permanent record.

The last requirement before we boarded the ship was to be interviewed by a psychiatrist. One by one, each soldier was directed to enter a room to see the doctor. When it was my turn, I knocked and went in. The army doctor was sitting behind a desk. I saluted and he halfheartedly returned the salute. He asked only one question: "Son do you want to go and fight?" My answer was, "Yes, Sir," and that was it.

We set sail in late October, 1943, and arrived in Liverpool on November 5. The voyage over was generally uneventful. The Empress of Australia had been a beautiful German ocean liner prior to the war. Somehow it had come into the hands of the British Government and now flew a British flag and had a British crew—and British food. I remember the sausage we had for breakfast tasted like sawdust with a little meat mixed in.

The supply sergeant liked my work and wanted to keep me there, but there was a war going on and I couldn't stay.

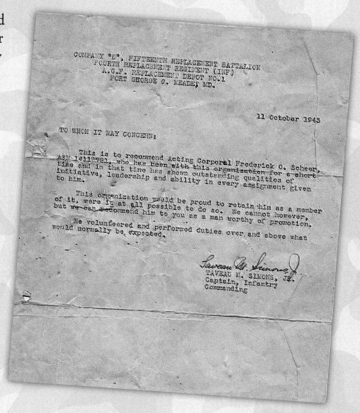

The ship was crowded with American soldiers going to join their combat units, stationed at the time in and around the British Isles. The sleeping arrangements were rather primitive. There were bunks and there were hammocks. Each bunk or hammock had to accommodate at least two soldiers, sometimes three—not all at once, of course, but consecutively. While one soldier was sleeping, the other two were off doing their own thing somewhere else. Unfortunately, many soldiers could not find places in the bunks or in the hammocks and found themselves sleeping restlessly on the deck and in the passageways. It was rather balmy for the end of October and the early part of November, probably because we were sailing eastward along the famous warm waters of the Gulf Stream. So, disdaining the passageways, as well as the bunks and hammocks, I elected to sleep for the entire five days of the trip on the open deck, where I claimed a comfortable spot as my own.

Each soldier was responsible for the full set of field equipment that had been issued to him at Fort Meade. There were no central areas for storage, so each soldier had to keep his material on or about his person. We would keep our rifles, backpacks, bayonets, and all the other stuff that had been issued to us close by where we slept. Two members of the Construction Battalion, known as CBs, were camped out near my spot on deck. These people were civilians under the control of the Navy. They would go into hostile areas to build bridges or other types of construction or in some cases as demolition teams to help the troops. They were essentially civilian engineers, and they did a hell of a job for the soldiers. They would often come under fire. I had never heard of this civilian group before, but I gained an immediate respect for them.

I do not recollect whether there were any showers aboard the ship, or whether we were able to take a bath of any kind. I do remember that I had no trouble with seasickness. I did, however, have just a little trouble learning to smoke a pipe with harsh tobacco in it, which gave me a little queasiness from time to time. When this would happen, I would make my way to the bow of the ship and let the wind blow in my face for a few minutes, and I would be all right.

It was dark when the ship arrived on November 5th, 1943. We boarded troop trains for the short trip to Feasey Farms, a mobilization and transshipment center just outside of Liverpool. Our group would be there only two days. I had heard about London fog but had never imagined fog like the fog we experienced at Feasey Farms. It was so thick that you could hold your arm out in front of you and not be able to see beyond your elbow.

I mentioned earlier how we learned to enjoy short friendships. Well, a guy in my bunk room and I became buddies. We found a deck of playing cards and decided to play Las Vegas-style Solitaire. It went like this: He would sell me the deck for $52.00. I would go through it one card at a time and he would pay me $1.00 for every usable card I turned up; then we would switch places. I ended up owing him about $3500.00, but it didn't matter because I never saw him again.

When we shipped out again, it would be to Warrenpoint, County Down, Northern Ireland, to join the 5th Infantry Division, Company C of the 2nd Infantry Regiment.

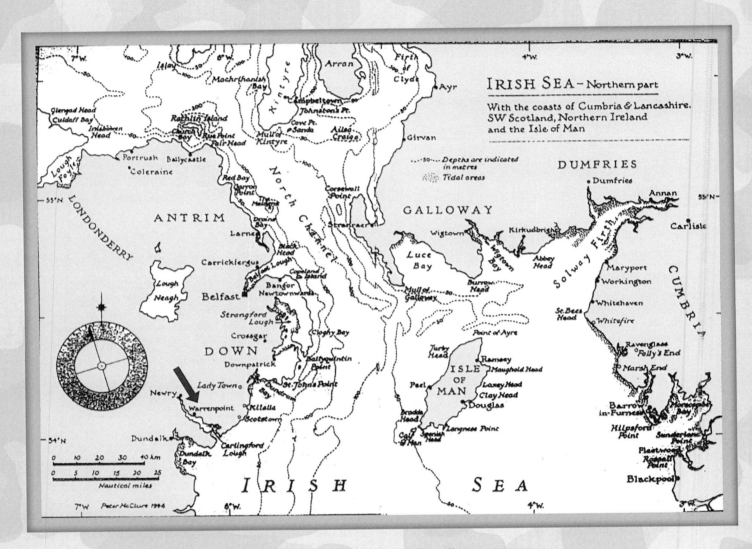

The arrow shows the location
of Warrenpoint, County Down,
Northern Ireland.

CHAPTER FOUR
Warrenpoint

Warrenpoint is a beautiful seacoast town nestled beside a major loch in County Down on the southeast coast of Northern Ireland. Northern Ireland, sometimes referred to as Ulster, is part of the United Kingdom. Southern Ireland, the Irish Free State, is a separate country and is not a part of the UK.[1] Ulster was as much a part of the Allied war effort as any other part of the U.K. The Irish Free State claimed neutrality, although many people, myself included, felt it was pro-German.

There were thousands of American soldiers billeted in and around Warrenpoint. My particular group was quartered in a civilian house, formerly a public guest house. The three-story building had been divided into two sections, one occupied by the civilians who apparently owned the house and the other given over to our platoon of some 35 to 40 men. Compared to the quarters aboard ship, the billeting in Warrenpoint was very comfortable indeed.

Having now been assigned to a unit, I got to know my companions and found them to be an interesting collection of men. Some were regular army, but many had been in that group of U.S. draftees who had been called up back in 1940 to serve for one year and had had their fate sealed when Pearl Harbor was bombed by Japan while they were on active duty.

The 5th Division was the first American army unit to see duty in the European Theater of Operations (ETO). The division had been assembled at Ft. Dix, New Jersey and shipped over to Iceland, where the men were stationed for about sixteen months before being sent to London. While the 5th was in Iceland, other units were shipped to England and other U.S. forces joined the British in the North African campaign. The men spent most of their time in Iceland pulling guard duty, unloading ships bringing supplies to Iceland and reloading those supplies onto other ships headed for Murmansk, Russia. Any remaining time was used to build or enlarge the camp, or just to goof off.

---

1 Ireland and Britain joined to become the UK in 1801. In 1921, 26 counties of Ireland left the union and became the Irish Free State (later the Irish Republic) and six Irish counties remained in the union as Northern Ireland.

These guys told many stories about their stay in Iceland. The camp was close to Reykjavik, so they often went into town when they had free time. It seems that male soldiers the world over, including the men of the 5th Division, have one common interest: women. There were lots of pretty girls in Reykjavik, Iceland—at least the guys thought they were pretty, until they smiled and you could see they had no teeth. A lack of calcium in their diet had caused this effect on the girls; the effect it caused on the GIs was to turn them off.

The second most common interest among GIs is food—especially baked goods. The guys would seek out a bakery and purchase some mouth-watering item they saw in the showcase. For those in the know, it was a great laugh to see an unsuspecting GI bite into his delicious-looking morsel and watch his expression change instantly from joyful to jaundiced. *Everything* in Iceland tasted like fish. The locals cooked with whale oil.

Nevertheless, free time was boring. Even playing poker and shooting craps would get old, so the men were always looking for ways to occupy themselves. From time to time they would come across pieces of aluminum from German airplanes that had been shot down. Someone came up with the idea to fashion these pieces into jewelry, using bits of colored plastic cut from toothbrush handles as stones. As time went on they became quite skilled at making mementos out of the aluminum scraps and toothbrushes. Their favorite items were rings, bracelets and pieces that could be worn on cords around the neck.

Without girls and food, there was little in Iceland for the guys of the 5th to spend their money on. A few sent some money home, but most of them simply saved it. They were eventually transferred to a small area just outside of London where they were able to spend it with abandon. When they arrived in the London area, the perfume of easy money and GIs with a big need for female favors attracted the attention of the "ladies of the evening" of Piccadilly Circus and Mayfair. These girls would cling to the men like guys were going out of style. In fact they were going out of style—or at least out of reach. The 5th Division was in the London area for only about two weeks before it shipped out to Northern Ireland. The story is that within 24 hours after their arrival there was not a pub anywhere in Warrenpoint that had a drop of alcohol left in it. These guys had consumed it all.

For the most part the pubs in Warrenpoint were dark and cool; at the same time, they offered a sense of quiet comfort. Their specialties seemed to be Old Bushmills Whiskey and Guinness Stout. There were always some old men sitting around drinking their pints of Guinness and mumbling to each other. I didn't understand anything they were talking

This postcard shows a general view of Warrenpoint.

about, but I am sure they did. I don't think they liked the Yanks very much, but they never said so; they just looked the other way most of the time. As for the food in the pubs, you could depend on the sausage. It was always good, made with a bit too much cereal perhaps, but good. There was also rabbit and chips—not fish or chicken and chips . . . rabbit. It was available in all the pubs, and it was good.

When we arrived in our new company area, we were ordered to line up outside company headquarters for inspection by the commanding officer and the first sergeant. We found out later that everyone thought our company commander was a first class SOB. He was a former Civilian Conservation Corps (CCC) camp commander. Our first sergeant was a massive man and a very tough soldier indeed—and his presence alone commanded respect.

After the CO made his "unwelcome" speech, the first sergeant looked us over from head to toe, both to size us up to see what kind of soldiers he had been given, and to set us straight on our future in Company C. When his gaze landed on me, he pointed a finger at those two stripes on my arm and said in a very unfriendly voice, "What are you doing with those stripes?" I said, "Sir, I don't know". He immediately reached up and tore them off my sleeve. I learned the hard way that "salt-water corporal" was not an actual rank, and no more was said about stripes.

My bunk was on the second floor in the room where the monthly payday craps game took place, and it seemed that the bottom panel of my bunk was the best place to use as a bumper. I didn't shoot craps; I had never learned how, but the shouting and the banging of the dice against the bottom of my bunk kept me awake most of every payday night. Among the regulars to these games was a guy named Hager who was an expert marksman—a skill he probably developed while shooting squirrels back in the hills of West Virginia. When off duty, this fellow would do nothing but go to chow and lie on his bunk. But on payday there was always the big craps game in our room as soon as chow was over and Hager was always there. He would stay until all of his money was gone; then he would crawl back onto his bunk until the next payday.

Another member of the platoon was great big Polish kid who came from somewhere in Pennsylvania. Immediately upon arrival, this fellow was assigned a Browning Automatic Rifle (BAR) to master, love, and use in combat. He thus became the BAR man in our platoon. The rifle had a much larger ammunition clip than the M-1 rifle I had been issued and could be fired on full automatic. The BAR was one heavy piece of equipment, and this guy was the horse to carry it.

. . . . .

We spent the following eight months in various types of combat training. Physical fitness, of course, was most important, and there were various types of physical exercise, including frequent hikes. This part of Northern Ireland was not at all like Kansas. The topography was rolling hills, some of which were quite steep. The hills were not mountains by any stretch of the imagination, but with a full field pack they were a rough climb. We continued to receive instruction in using our rifles and bayonets, throwing hand grenades, and hand-to-hand combat. This was an infantry unit and our training focused on the duties an infantryman would be expected to perform in combat.

One morning we were out on a wide open grassy area with rolling hills and valleys practicing bayonet thrusts at one another and using the butts of our rifles on each other's heads. Suddenly the Platoon Lieutenant arrived in a jeep and came bolting up to the sergeant, shouting and waving his arms, yelling, "What are you doing? Are you trying to get some of these men killed?" It seems the sergeant had us drilling using naked bayonets. "Have them sheath those bayonets immediately!!" I was sure there was going to be a fist fight between the lieutenant and the sergeant after the sergeant shouted back, "These men have got to know what danger is. Someday they will be fighting with open blades and it won't be a game." There was no fist fight, but the lieutenant won and we sheathed our bayonets. We had never seen a sergeant shout at a lieutenant before; we just stood there with our mouths hanging open in disbelief.

One day we were practicing throwing hand grenades at this same training area. We learned there were different types of grenades. First was the old favorite that looks like a pineapple. There was also a concussion grenade, but by far the most spectacular was the white phosphorus grenade. When the white phosphorus grenade exploded, it sent tiny pieces of phosphorus flying in all directions. It was said that, if a piece landed on your arm, it would immediately burn right through. At a distance, though, the detonation looked like a beautiful white shooting star.

. . . . .

The house in which our unit was billeted sat on a main street along the waterfront. From the front of the house you could see the sea wall and Carlingford Lough. The seawall had a sidewalk beside it that went on for miles. People spent hours walking along it.

One afternoon after duty hours, I went out for a walk, also known as "cruising for girls," along the wall. As I was going my merry way, I spotted a beautiful young Irish colleen. Not being the bashful type, I tried to start a conversation with her, but she would have none of it. The next night I went for another walk, this time on the lookout for the same young lady. There she was again, walking along the seawall, head up, not looking to the left or right, and appearing as cool as a cucumber to anyone around—especially a Yank. But my mother always said that when I wanted something, I was so persistent that sooner or later I would get it—and I wanted this young lady. Sure enough, after a while she decided it was safe to stop and talk to me. Her name was Nellie, she was about my own age and, as I said before, she was good looking. It was not long before we were meeting most evenings to walk along the seawall. Then one evening she suggested that, since the next day was Saturday and my platoon would be off duty, perhaps I would come to her house for tea.

Nellie lived with her cousins, Mr. and Mrs. B., who turned out to be what I considered old people, but nice. (I was only 19, so anyone over 50 was old to me.) It happened that their house was almost directly behind our billet, on the next street over. To reach it you had to walk up the street about a hundred yards, take a left turn up an alley and another left turn down the street to her house. I thought the house was very quaint. It was a small, two-story house typical of the neighborhood. It was neat and clean and the couple had undoubtedly lived there for a long time. This was the first time I had ever seen a house lighted by gas lights. The lights were lit by coal gas piped in and metered just as natural gas is today—except that the meters did not run continuously, but worked more like parking meters. One of my most unforgettable experiences was watching the lights start to dim and seeing someone rush to put a penny in the meter to brighten them up again.

Mrs. B. was a talkative person with a quick wit and a warm laugh. She was a tall, lanky woman; her husband was tall, lean and balding. Mr. B. was a bit more worldly, having been to the US in the 1920s to work in a watch factory, but hadn't liked it and had come back to Ireland. He didn't have much to say, but Mrs. B. would tell stories about Ireland or describe events in Irish history, a subject that was completely unfamiliar to me. I learned about the wars between the Orangemen and the Rose Men, the same factions that continued to fight for control of Northern Ireland until the Belfast Agreement was signed in 1998. The only difference is that they are referred to now as the Catholics and the Protestants. I still can't remember which ones were the Orangemen and which were the Rose Men.[2]

The table was set for only two. Mrs. B. made herself scarce, but Mr. B. walked through the dining room, looked at the little sandwiches, sweet scones and tea and in a very dry voice said, "Looks like pre-war."

I quickly became a frequent visitor to that house. In fact, I was there whenever I was off duty, but not for the food. Nellie and I fell very much in love and the family always made me feel welcome. One night I took Nellie to the USO center in town where we found ourselves doing the Hokey-Pokey with a large group of other GIs and their dates. Remember the Hokey-Pokey? Nowadays children learn it in preschool, but back then it was new[3] and quite popular in clubs. I learned to do the Hokey-Pokey that night in Warrenpoint, County Down, Northern Ireland.

---

2   The Orangemen, known today as Unionists, were named for William III of Orange, the Dutch prince who became King of England in 1689, are predominantly Protestant, and favor political and cultural union with England. Rose (Ross) Men, generally Catholic, fought for an independent Irish nation and are now referred to as Nationalists.

3   The history of the Hokey-Pokey is bedeviled by accusations of plagiarism, but the original seems to have been composed by Jimmy Kennedy in the UK in 1942 and was referred to during the War years variously as the *Cokey-Cokey*, the *Okey-Cokey* and the *Hokey-Cokey*. The US version under the name *Hokey-Pokey* is usually attributed to Larry LaPrise and was copyrighted in 1949.

Not only was I very fond of Nellie, but also I thought Mrs. B. was a real prize. One evening I was asking what she thought of then Prime Minister Winston Churchill. She laughed and asked if I knew that Mr. Churchill once had to escape from a Belfast banquet hall in a fireman's uniform. It seems that he had been asked to make a speech at a banquet in his honor and while the banquet was in progress, word arrived that members of the militant Irish Republican Army (IRA) were out to get him. Hearing this, someone went out and borrowed a uniform from a fireman friend. As those assembled were being served desert, Mr. Churchill excused himself to use the restroom. He entered the gentlemen's lounge, donned the uniform, quietly slipped out a side entrance and escaped safely back to London.

From time to time I received packages from home and would share some of the goodies with Nellie and her cousins. My folks often included a copy of the *Saturday Evening Post* or some other magazine that they thought I would enjoy. Mrs. B. wasn't interested in the news or other articles in American magazines, but she thought the ads were wonderful and loved to pore over them again and again. In addition, Mother would occasionally go to the local do-it-yourself cannery in Eatonton and put up some home-roasted pecans. You can imagine how these went over with the Bs. Even Mr. B., who usually had little to say, commented on how good they were and wanted to know what kind of nuts grew with salt on them. Mother would also can some good old country fried chicken. This was a mouth-watering treat, but it made me a little homesick.

This postcard shows the building where I was billeted. Across the street is the seawall with its walkway where Nelly and I met and spent many evening hours.

It was quite cold in Warrenpoint in the winter of 1944. Although there was no snow that winter, there was frequently very heavy frost. Sometimes it appeared to be about an inch thick, but if you scraped the frost away you could look underneath and see the heather that seemed to always be green. Mr. B. often remarked that the weather in Ireland was particularly bad that year because of all the bombing on the continent. Evidently he had insight into the scientific determination of weather patterns and how they were affected by explosive devices. The fact was that the weather in Warrenpoint that winter was no different than it was before or after the war, and no different from what it is today. Another of Mr. B's frequent comments was, "Those Yanks. All they do is walk about and stick out their arms to look at their watches." Mr. B., of course, carried a pocket watch.

Another treat the GIs discovered was the barbershop. The barber was a friendly fellow with brown, slightly graying hair that was long and bushy and stood up on the top of his head. Most of us had not been shaving for very long and were not particularly good at it, so when we learned we could get a shave for the large sum of ten pence—about forty cents in US money at the time—we suddenly became big spenders.

I have several other fond memories of my stay in Warrenpoint, including a vivid recollection of the house in which our unit was billeted. Some 45 years later my wife Gerry and I visited Dublin in Southern Ireland and took a day trip to Northern Ireland and Warrenpoint. Shortly after we arrived, while I was walking around trying to get oriented, a little old man approached us and asked if we were Americans. When I told him that yes, we were, he stuck out his hand and introduced himself and told me how to find the old guest house and some other places. Then he asked me if I knew Mike O'Brien. He said I must know Mike because he had been here in 1944, and has come back almost every year since. In fact, he said, Mike has a bar in New York and surely everyone in

This photo was taken when Gerry and I visited Warrenpoint in 1989.

America must know him. Well, I didn't (and still don't), but I never did convince him and we went our way without our new Irish friend.

The old house that had been my home for nine months during the war was still there. We also looked for the house where Nellie had lived with her cousins and I think we were about to find it when I got a little embarrassed because Gerry started teasing me, so I steered our search in the other direction. We also learned that the railroad station where our mess hall had been located had been demolished and was now a container port. There had definitely been some changes made to this little town in the 45 years I had been away.

As we walked around the streets of Warrenpoint, we selected a place to have lunch. While we were eating, I asked an old man sitting at a nearby table several questions about the town in 1944. To my surprise he did not answer me. The waitress asked him my questions again; he answered her and she repeated his answers to me. (Maybe he couldn't understand my accent or maybe he just didn't talk to strangers, but I think it was probably the accent.) I asked about Nellie and her cousins, but he had no knowledge of them. I did learn the history of the building in which we were having lunch. In 1944 it had been a clinic for dispensing prophylactics to the soldiers. It had also been used as a treatment center for those soldiers who had selected the wrong date for an evening and had been rewarded with an unwelcome social disease. Now though, it was just another old house converted into a family restaurant.

THE U.S. FORCES IN ULSTER

Special Easter Services

Arrangements for Easter religious services for United States soldiers of all faiths stationed in Northern Ireland have been completed.

Protestant and Roman Catholic services will be conducted in and near Belfast for all troops under the Northern Ireland Base Section Command and at all S.O.S. installations throughout Ulster. Jewish Passover services will be held at the Jewish Institute, Belfast, to-night, to-morrow, and on Sunday night. Rabbi Herman Dicker, Cincinnati, Ohio, the only American Jewish chaplain in Ulster, and Rabbi Cecil M. Block, chaplain of all British Forces in the Province, will conduct the services, which will be attended by soldiers from all units, British and American, as well as members of all other Allied nations.

The American Red Cross and other organisations have provided sleeping facilities, and some units have arranged special trains to enable troops to attend.

Protestant services will be held at headquarters on Sunday at 11 a.m. by Chaplain William T. Brundick, of Woodstock, Virginia. Brigadier-General Leroy P. Collins, Commanding General, will attend. There will also be a special Lutheran communion service on Sunday at 4-30 p.m. at Carlisle Memorial Methodist Church, Belfast.

Roman Catholic services will be conducted by Chaplain Matthew Meghin, of Booker, New York, at St. Bridget's Church, Belfast, to-day and on Sunday. On Sunday a choir of 40 boys from St. Colordo's Monastery, will lead the praise. In addition, Easter masses will be celebrated at Belfast Barracks at 10 a.m. and at the "Nibs" guard-house at 11 a.m.

Services have also been arranged at Armagh, Omagh, and Newcastle.

This notice announces plans for Easter and Passover observances for the troops.

Passover in Northern Ireland 1944

The following is an attempt to give a report of our Passover activities. This is very difficult, but we will try to cover the main features.

Place: It was clear to us from the beginning that a holiday like Passover could only be celebrated where there was a Jewish community of any size. The choice was easy since Belfast is the only city in Northern Ireland that fits this description. The Jewish Institute in Belfast is a two story building erected in 1927. It has a hall on the second floor which seats approximately 400. The ground floor has smaller rooms with a combined seating capacity of 150. It was built to suit the social activities of a community of 300 families.

Attendance: How many will come? This was our second problem. We knew that it would be impossible to accommodate all the troops at once. A separation according to branch of service, units and geographic location was necessary and orders to that effect were issued. This required co-ordination between the various Headquarters of Services of Supply, Army Ground Forces, Air Forces and Navy. The basic idea behind it was that each soldier, stationed in Ulster, should have at least one Seder. Our first figure, later substantiated by facts, estimated an approximate attendance of 2000 men at one time or another during Passover Services. The co-operation of the military authorities was excellent.

Utensils: We could hardly expect to serve the wine, Knedlach and other Passover dishes in GI Mess Kits and Cups; it would have reduced the festive spirit to a great extent. We, therefore, contacted our Quartermaster who obtained from various sources, British Ordnance and Civilian, the following items: 100 sheets, 500 knives, 500 forks, 1000 spoons, 3 carving knives and forks, 3 butcher knives, steels, 3 ladles, 500 small glasses (Port), 500 tumblers, 1000 soup plates, 500 dinner plates, 500 desert plates, 200 cups, 200 saucers, 200 teaspoons, 4 stoves (field), 3 eight-gallon boilers, 6 four-gallon dixies, 12 baking dishes, 6 large iron saucepans, 80 forms and 30 trestle tables.

Food: Matzoh, wine and meal were easy to get. John Sills, Jewish Welfare Board, London, early in March shipped us 1 ton of Matzoh, 200 quarts of wine and 200 pounds of meal. Rationed items, such as meat etc, were not easily obtainable. Special request had to be made to the Ministry of Food. At this point we have to mention Mr. L. Hyman, J. P. 755 Antrim Road, Belfast, the Chairman of our Hospitality Committee. His tireless efforts and wholehearted co-operation were greatly responsible for the success of our arrangements. Without Mr. Hyman, no Pessach of such style could have been celebrated in Northern Ireland.

Home Hospitality and Sleeping Accommodations: The bulk of the personnel slept at the American Red Cross. Those who were taken care of by the Home Hospitality, which amounted to approximately 400, did not have to worry. We may add that members of the Hospitality Committee had previously canvassed the community as to the number of available homes. There was hardly a Jewish home in Northern Ireland - there are a few smaller towns with Jewish people - which did not invite two or more to its Seder. These people truly lived up to the Passover spirit, shared their rations with their guests and felt honored by the Americans at their table.

Holidays: We were slightly nervous and anxious when the holidays approached. Could we satisfy our boys from Brooklyn and the Bronx? Would our services, of which we had four, including morning worship with the readings of the Torah, be of a nature to be enjoyed by everybody? Would the long absence from home for some troops, or the first Passover overseas for others, influence the festive spirit? Then they came, officers and men, critical, reserved and expectant. Soon the ice broke. British and American soldiers mingled freely and became friends. Many recognized their old buddies with whom they had grown up and whom they had not seen for many years. Two brothers met, one a Captain and the other a Private. The air vibrated with joy and happiness. A true holiday was born.

Rev. C. M. Bloch, The British Chaplain, assisted very ably in the conduct of the Seder and the Services. Upstairs, we could extend the length of our Seder, tell more of the Hagadah and sing more songs. Downstairs, we had to shorten things in order to get through with two and three Sedarim at the same time. Everyone had a Hagadah before him so that he could follow. The Mah Nishtanah contained new questions Why all this war, why away from home, why in Ulster and how long was it going to last? Some questions had to remain open, but many could be answered.

The food, which had been prepared by our own cooks, was plentiful and delicious. Four American and one British operated for five days 4 field kitchens, burned 70 gallons of gas and helped the civilian chefs; 7 waitresses and 2 waiters served. The wine was more symbolic than tasty. Everyone had about two ounces. Its color was traditionally red, but the shipment to Ulster and the crossing of the Irish sea did not increase its strength. Nevertheless, we all had a good time. Too bad that the Army photographer was unlucky and only one picture was successful. For instance, none of the scenes, showing the Chaplains together with members of all branches of the American and British Forces or the one railway station with the special troop train of 400 men from one unit, were taken. Especially true was this of their return, most of them with Matzah packages under their arm.

We could go on and on, simply because it is enjoyable for the writer reviewing all the happy scenes again. No doubt, many points have been overlooked and many obstacles could not be disclosed. But to sum up, we may say, it was the biggest and best Passover celebration we have ever seen. Let us hope and pray that it will strengthen our spirit and help our mind till the day of our final return. May it be soon.

Herman Dicker
HERMAN DICKER
Chaplain,
US Army.

I didn't know they would have Passover services in Ireland, but they did. The army provided transportation and I went. Chaplain Herman Dicker filed this report.

Northern Ireland's landscape of rolling hills is covered with a low growing tough plant known as heather. The various plots of land are separated by stone walls, similar to the ones sometimes seen in New England. The stones had been removed from the fields to allow for cultivation and stacked to form borders between one field and another. The roots of the heather, which abounded in these fields, matted together to form peat and the fields were frequently mined for the peat. The foliage would be cut away and the roots extracted in squares to form blocks of peat about six inches thick. The blocks were dried and became the principal fuel for heating and cooking in many of the farm houses in Ireland.

Our days and many of the nights in the Warrenpoint area were spent in training for the combat that was sure to come. Night training exercises were a standard diet. On many occasions—in fact on most occasions—when the American soldiers were positioned at night in the hill country surrounding Warrenpoint, they would seek out a civilian farmhouse, go there, and buy hard-boiled eggs. It seems that the Irish farmers, always entrepreneurs, had discovered that American soldiers liked hot hard-boiled eggs and made a practice of having eggs hot, ready, and waiting by the dozens when the American soldiers would appear. A dozen eggs went for about a one pound note, which would have been about $4.00 at that point in time. To most of us a one pound note just felt like a dollar bill and we spent them the same way. The nights out on those hills were cold and the warmth and taste of the eggs were a delight for all of us. And anyway, we were using what seemed to us to be play money.

IRISH VILLAGE SCENE.

The farmhouses we would visit on our training exercises looked very much like the one depicted on this postcard.

On one particular evening our group, probably two or three platoons, set out in the hills on a night problem. We had been proceeding for some time in a long single-file line over the hills and across the stone walls. It was quite dark at this point, with no moonlight to help light the way. As we marched through the hills, we would frequently encounter one of the walls, generally about four feet high and 18 to 24 inches wide. Each of us in turn would crawl over it and we would continue in single file. As I was crawling over one of these walls, my rifle slipped out of my hands and dropped over ahead of me. I quickly regained my balance and my rifle and hurried to catch up with the guy in front of me. He seemed to be taking a strange twist from the direction that we had been going, but I thought he was following the noncom in the lead. Actually, we were heading toward Southern Ireland. (Remember, County Down was on the border of Southern Ireland, the Irish Free State.) Then, as best I could make out, he took a strange little hop just as I caught up to him. "Him" was not quite the word for it. I had been following a sheep, and we were heading straight for Southern Ireland! Fortunately for me a little moonlight appeared and I was able to spot the real soldier, correct my direction and avoid leading the whole group of American soldiers behind me into Southern Ireland—a neutral country—and possibly internment until the end of the war.

Another memory of Warrenpoint that should be recorded is the suspicious nature of some of the Irish men in the area. Near our mess hall was something akin to a town square. Occasionally a GI would drive his tank into this area, park it, and go to lunch. Often a small Irish man, a cigarette dangling from his lip and a cap pulled down over his brow, would walk around the tank examining each and every detail with considerable attention. He could have been a member of the Irish Republican Army (IRA) or simply a sympathetic civilian. Many of the soldiers suspected that these individuals were, in fact, operatives of the IRA and that they were providing whatever information they could gather to the Germans. It was well known that the Irish Free State was sympathetic to the German cause.

One day two of us received orders to accompany an ammunition train to Londonderry in the north of Ulster in the county of Londonderry. In charge of our ammunition detail was buck sergeant by the name of Tandy. Now if you think Frederick "O'Scheer," was a great name to have in Ireland, you should try Tandy. Irish tradition holds that Saint Napper Tandy had run all the snakes out of Ireland, so surely anyone with that name must be his kin. To his credit, Sergeant Tandy was young and good looking and all the Irish lassies wanted him for their own, saint kin or not.

It was a short train, just an engine and tender, two boxcars and a caboose. Whenever the train stopped, my mate and I would jump down from the caboose and walk around the train to protect it from I don't know what. The trip was mostly uneventful, however at one stop we were told that we were to wait beside a switching station while the engine was switched off and replaced with another one. It was cold standing there among the tracks, and we were beginning to shiver, so the sergeant took pity on us and went into the little tower that housed the switching station and got permission for us to come in and warm up. We were told that, under no circumstances, were we to touch anything and we didn't. But it was tempting. It was the great big levers—a whole row of them—that the trainman shifted to switch tracks that tempted us. Gosh that looked like fun. You could have trains going all over the place just by moving a few of those levers. The sergeant saw my buddy gazing at those levers and beginning to move in their direction, and we were hustled out of there before we could cause a disaster. We had only stayed a couple of minutes, but it was great.

When we arrived at Londonderry we were relieved of our train and told to go to the Navy mess hall for breakfast before returning to Warrenpoint. We went into mess hall, got trays from the stack and started through the line. We couldn't believe our eyes—these guys lived like kings! There were eggs—as many as you wanted—cooked any way you wanted, while you stood and waited. The cook on the other side of the steam counter even smiled. Then there were the standard items: bacon, American-style sausage, toast, jam, butter that would melt and great coffee. What were we doing in the Army?

Well, good things always come to an end and we headed back to Warrenpoint. This time we rode in the coach of the train not the caboose. Remember our good-looking Sergeant Tandy? The train we were riding on was a civilian train and the Irish girls riding in that train car couldn't keep their hands off him. All my partner and I could do was turn green with envy.

. . . . .

The invasion of France by the Allied Forces had commenced on June 6, 1944, with amphibious landings on and east of the Cherbourg Peninsula in the Normandy area of France. All of us were on pins and needles. We had heard that the Americans, the British, the Canadians and the Free French had invaded the European continent on the northern coast of France.

In the following days the pace of training quickened and anxiety became the rule of the day. During this time the 5th Division had a very special guest: General George F. Patton, Jr., at that time the commander of the Third Army of which the 5th Division was a part. As would be expected in anticipation of a visit from a general of his stature, it was proper for the troops to stand around in a loose formation awaiting his arrival. We were out in the sun in an open field and as it got hotter and hotter, some of the guys amused themselves by playing volleyball with little white balloons they had made—from condoms.

General Patton arrived and mounted a specially prepared platform, his four bodyguards stationing themselves at the corners. Each guard stood facing us, holding a Tommy gun at the ready. The general gave his famous standard pep talk to the soldiers of the 5th Division, urging them to be brave and to remember that, "You can't dig your way up a hill; you have to charge it!" He seemed to look directly into the soldiers' eyes and as he shifted his body and talked, we could see the sun gleaming off the highly polished pearl-handled pistols he wore on each hip. I don't know which had the higher shine, his boots or his pistols. The speech was short and to the point. When he was finished, he clicked his heels and the command "ATTENTION" rang out from every bar and stripe that had vocal cords. We snapped to and the brass gave a sharp salute. Without another word the general returned the salute, turned, and departed the reviewing stand with his bodyguards falling in, in step, two in front and two in the rear.

It was interesting that for a week or more following the Patton's speech, tongue-in-cheek memos came down from Division HQ through our Company Command, saying in effect that parts of the general's speech were obviously "bullshit," and to disregard them. They didn't say which parts.

The soldiers of the 5th Division were ready. They knew that their time was soon to come and it soon did.

V-mail was sent to and from the soldiers overseas. After the letters were cleared by the censors, they were copied to microfilm and then printed in reduced size to conserve shipping space. Considering the size of the armed forces, there was an enormous amount of mail.

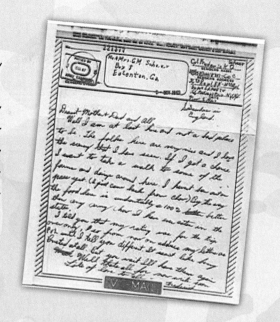

Over the next few days, gossip about what was going on in France was rife. Many of the soldiers said they wished they could have taken part in the initial invasion just so that they could have seen what it was like.

During these last days of training another member of my platoon and I were issued a special grenade launcher that fit onto our M-1s. The launcher is a metal tube that fits over the barrel of the rifle. A rifle grenade is a football-shaped object about 1½ inches in diameter and two to three inches long mounted on a 12-inch staff with fins. The grenade staff fits over the launcher and is fired by a blank 30-caliber round. Rifle grenades are fired from a standing position with the butt of the rifle against the shoulder, or from a kneeling position with the toe of the rifle butt on the ground. The kneeling position was considerably preferred because a rifle kicks like a mule when launching a grenade.

Thus we became grenade launchers for our platoon. But we received almost no training; only once were we taken to a remote area and permitted to fire a grenade. We each put a launcher on our rifle, loaded a blank round in the chamber and fired. We all watched as the grenades lofted toward an imaginary target. Afterwards we were issued carrying bags holding six rifle grenades and blank ammunition to launch them. This practice shot was the only time I ever used the grenade launcher.

For several days we were on alert for shipping out to France. We had been restricted to our quarters in the divided three-story house until further notice. Once or twice the order came down to pack our gear and be ready to fall out in two hours, but before the two hours had passed, we were told to stand down, restore our gear and wait. This went on for over a week. Other than to go to mess or sick call, we could not leave the building.

One mid-morning while cleaning my rifle for the fifteenth time, one of the guys stuck his head in our door and said someone wanted to see me downstairs at the back door. I had no idea what was going on, but the only way to find out was to go down and see—and he had said to hurry, so I did. When I got to the back door of our building, I saw a fellow standing by the wooden wall that separated the two halves of the back yard. He put his finger to his lips as if to say, "Don't talk, just come over here." When they had said keep to quarters they meant it, so during this time of waiting I had not been able to see Nellie. When I looked over the wall, there she was waiting for me so she could say good-bye. Not needing any further explanation, I vaulted over the wall and you can imagine what a glorious good-bye we had in the next few minutes. It seems the civilians who lived in the other side of the building had arranged for some of us to say good-bye to our sweethearts. They had allotted only a few minutes for each of us and under the circumstances that had to do. This had to be done very secretively; if the brass had known about it, both we and the civilians would have been in big trouble. But what a sweet good-bye it was.

I never saw Nellie again. Ours was a story played out hundreds of times by young lovers like us who were drawn together in the urgency of the war years, our lives changed by being so deeply in love and then so abruptly separated. For the men and women on foreign soil, those deep feelings were soon eroded by their thoughts of home. All of those heartfelt vows faded to shadows and dreams.

Finally, the order came down to pack up and ship out. We assembled on the street with our packs and equipment. Strangely enough, our route to the rail station took us around the rear of our building and down the street where Nellie lived. I didn't see her though, and I'll never know if she saw me. We boarded a troop train and proceeded to an Irish port and on to France. We were among thousands of young soldiers aboard massive troop ships headed toward the beaches of Normandy. We arrived on July 10, 1944.

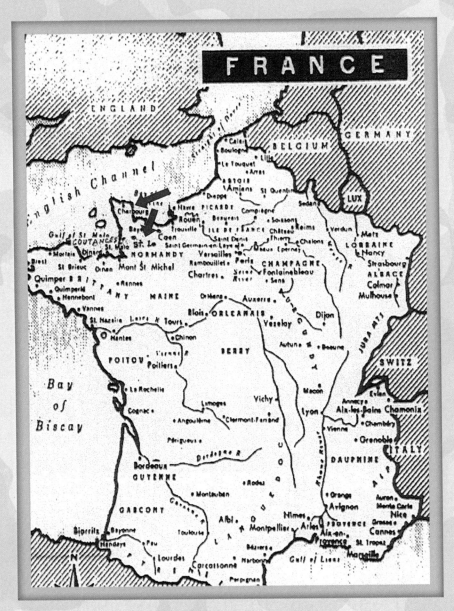

This map shows the Cherbourg Peninsula with the towns of St. Lo and Caen.

CHAPTER FIVE
Normandy

July 10th dawned bright and sunny off the Normandy coast. Ours was a darn big ship. Because of its size, it was forced to anchor far out from the beach. All over the area, there were ships offloading men and supplies onto landing craft that would ferry them to the beach and then return for another load. As each craft pull alongside the ship, the men were instructed to climb over the side with all their equipment and climb down a rope ladder onto the boat. And that was one unbelievable ladder! Imagine fishing net made of rope about an inch in diameter stretching nearly the entire length of the ship and reaching from the top of the gunwale to just above the landing craft deck. We had to crawl over the gunwale, get our footing in the rope, and work our way down the side of the ship—all while the ship was heaving to and fro, the landing craft was bobbing up and down and we were loaded down with all our gear. It may sound like fun, but it wasn't. None of us had ever performed this particular trick before, so this was quite an exhilarating event. The good news is that we were able to accomplish it without anyone falling into the water. The landing craft were jammed-packed with soldiers and gear. My boat had standing room only.

The landing craft proceeded toward the shore from the troop ship. When it grounded itself on the sandy beach, the great front gate was lowered to become a ramp, and all of us scrambled ashore onto dry land and formed up in the regular military formations of platoons and companies. This was Utah Beach; Omaha Beach was several miles to the east, with Gold, Juno and Sword beaches stretching further east beyond it. Although there was the noise of the ships and the landing craft plying back and forth, it seemed strangely quiet. There was no combat noise from the beaches; it had been a little over a month since the initial invasion. This entire area of the northern coast of France had been taken and secured by Allied Forces, who by now had worked their way a good distance inland toward the city of St. Lo.

The 5th Division soldiers were loaded onto trucks and transported toward St. Lo to relieve the forces of the 2nd Infantry Division, which had been a part of the original invasion force and had been in active combat for about a month. These units of the 2nd Division were relieved and, as far as I know, some were sent back to England for R & R and others went to support other parts of the 2nd Division at St. Lo. The 5th Division would occupy a region east of the city in the Caen sector that the 2nd Division had secured—an area that would become known as the "hedgerow" area of northern France. The countryside was similar in a way to that surrounding Warrenpoint where the fields had been divided by rock walls, except that while the Irish walls were built of field stones and were generally bare, the French hedgerows were earthen and were topped by a heavy growth of trees and bushes. The hedgerows divided the farm plots into giant squares of about eight or ten acres each. This was obviously farming country, and while there were farmhouses and farm animals—alive and dead—scattered across it, there were no French farmers in evidence. The hedgerows, however, were a substantial impediment to the movement of military forces, particularly mechanized forces. Eventually, heavy steel blades would be placed on the front of many of the tanks and other vehicles to enable them to navigate their way across the terrain. It was along this line of hedgerows that we settled in for 17 days before we would begin moving south.

The line that the 5th Division occupied was static, moving neither forward nor backward. It had been occupied previously by the 2nd Division and extended for several miles east and west near the southern end of the Cherbourg Peninsula, northwest of the city of St. Lo. The 5th Division had been assigned areas of control within the line. We were fortunate in one respect: As the 2nd Division soldiers moved out, they left behind their foxholes, which were immediately available for our comfort and safety. The holes extended all along the line from east to west and were usually positioned behind one of the hedgerows, which gave us additional protection. Each one was a unique architectural structure, designed according to the whims of the particular soldier who had dug it. I found one for myself that was about 4 feet deep, 5 or 6 feet long and about 3 feet wide—big enough for me to crouch down in when the unit came under fire. It is surprising how much a hole in the ground can feel like home when you get used to it. After a little while you start making little adjustments and adding features to enhance your comfort. For us, that might include some straw for bedding or other stuff we found around the farmyards. The weather was nice; it didn't rain for the whole 17 days we were there.

All was not peace and quiet during these few days, however. A great battle was being waged for St. Lo. American Forces had taken the town on several occasions, but had been driven back. German forces were arrayed in front of and south of the American forces and conducted frequent night patrols in, around, and through the hedgerows. It was not uncommon for German soldiers on night patrol to circle around the forward American outpost and send a barrage of small arms fire toward the American positions from the hedgerow behind us. They wanted us to return fire so that they could determine our location. Had we done so, our positions would have been readily visible to the German artillery spotters, who would have brought down a rain of 88-millimeter German artillery upon us. We had been strictly ordered not to fire our weapons, but to respond to any German attack only in a manner that would not divulge our specific location.

One night some of our guys violated these orders, but strangely enough, there was no resulting artillery barrage. The men had spotted a German patrol close to their foxholes and, being somewhat nervous about having Germans so nearby, they disregarded the order and fired. A terrific firefight ensued that went on for hours. Almost the entire night and early morning hours were consumed by our soldiers blasting away with their rifles and carbines at the Germans and the German soldiers blasting back at them. As the sun came up the firing quieted down and when it was possible to take a look at the field where the fight had taken place, we began to take stock of the damage. Surprisingly, we found no casualties. There were no dead or wounded German soldiers, nor were there any dead or wounded American soldiers. The only obvious casualties were two large hogs, which, to our great delight, became a barbecue. There was some speculation later as to whether the firefight had actually been between American troops and German troops. Some thought it might have been American troops on both sides of the firefight, but this was never determined.

Shortly after this incident we learned that a British reconnaissance unit had been brought in to secure our left flank. As was their custom, the German night patrols again came close by, challenging the British to respond to their fire so that they could call in their heavy artillery. The British, however, were not timid at all and did not adopt the American's practice. When the German patrol opened fire, the British sent flares up and opened up with everything they had, apparently obliterating the German patrol. Thereafter, not insignificantly, the Germans discontinued their nightly forays.

The comfort and protection of the foxholes was enhanced by the delicacy of the C-rations, which were our staple diet while in this stationary position. There were no field kitchens to provide any other food service. The C-ration came in a box about a foot square and about six inches deep. There were cheeses, some kind of bread or crackers and always some canned Spam, as well as other foods that did not need refrigeration, especially powdered milk—and Nescafé. I had never seen nor heard of powdered coffee that only required a little hot water to make a perfectly delightful cup of coffee. And the C-ration box always contained the all-important cigarettes—at least four packs, usually Lucky Strikes.

Menu from a C-ration box.

The guys in our platoon were quite innovative in devising ways to heat the water for coffee and shaving. It seems that the French farmer whose property we occupied was quite the wine maker. Being a lover of good wine, he had buried caches of Benedictine, a very heavy and potent French brandy, in various places near his home. When our guys discovered these stashes, they would unearth the Benedictine and use it for a variety of purposes—not only to drink, but also to clean their rifles, and to provide fuel for fires to boil water for coffee. The standard canteen cup and our steel helmets were great for boiling water. The cup was just right for making coffee and the steel helmet worked admirably as a washbasin for shaving.

Among the delicacies we found near the French farm house were chickens and the eggs they would leave. It was not at all unusual to see pairs of soldiers wandering among the farm buildings, one with his rifle at the ready, scanning the landscape and tree tops for snipers, and the other collecting eggs. Isn't this how armies have always fed themselves? It's known as *foraging*, which is the military term for stealing. Just as in Warrenpoint, we all loved our eggs hard-boiled and hot, which is how we cooked them in and around our foxholes.

. . . . .

Several incidents occurred during those 17 days. Once when a buddy and I were wandering through an apple orchard not far from our foxholes, we saw American and German aircraft above us engaged in a dogfight, just like we see in old World War II movies today. Sometimes when one of the planes was on a downward slope and shooting at one of the others, the machine gun bullets came perilously close to where we were, forcing us to dive for cover. Neither of us was hit, so no damage was done, but I'll never forget that moment.

Another time I was posted in a small farm house as part of a communications team. Our unit used landline telephones with wires connecting our headquarters to several different outpost locations. We were not using radio communications because the receivers at the outposts could give away our position. There was an incessant clicking noise on the line and the communications sergeant was convinced that the lines were being tapped by the Germans. It was more likely, though, that the clicking was caused by shells exploding in the area near the lines.

The third, and most dramatic, of the incidents that occurred during this period was the landing and explosion of a German buzz bomb about 2000 yards from my foxhole. A buzz bomb is an unguided missile that the Germans directed at England, but this one had misfired and landed in our area of northern France. The thing sounded like an old washing machine or a Model-A Ford passing overhead, but then the noise stopped abruptly and a few seconds later we heard the detonation. It was the most tremendous explosion I had ever heard and it sent dirt and flames rising into the sky. The next day some of us went over to see what had happened and found a crater that looked big enough to hold an American bungalow.

I also remember the sounds coming from American artillery being fired from behind our position toward the German lines. This was not a sometimes occurrence; it went on almost constantly. As the artillery shells passed overhead, they sounded like propellers gushing through a stream of water—a sort of purring sound—eerie, but reassuring because it meant that our artillery was giving a constant dose of big lead to the Jerries.

. . . . .

A strange and unusual incident occurred during this period. Early one morning after I had finished standing watch, I started to remove the bayonet from my rifle. The bayonet stuck and was difficult to remove. I leaned over it and jerked on it several times. As I gave it one more little jerk, it suddenly released and hit me on the forehead just above my nose and right between the eyes. The company medic took me to the battalion aid station, where the station commander took a look and decided to make as complete an examination as possible under the conditions of the aid station. It was soon ascertained that the wound to my forehead was not serious and I was returned to duty. From his examination however, the doctor determined that I suffered from night blindness caused by retinitis pigmentosa. This was the first indication that I had a problem with my vision, other than the astigmatism for which I had worn glasses for most of my life. Upon reflection though, I did remember times when I had had difficulty seeing at night, but I thought it was a characteristic common to everyone. I didn't think anyone could see at night.

When I returned to my unit I delivered the memo from the medic informing my commanding officer that I had night blindness and was not to be assigned any night duties. My commanding officer was outraged and said in no uncertain terms, "I have seen people with headaches, with backaches, with foot aches and all kinds of other maladies wanting to be relieved from duty, but I have never heard of anyone with night blindness! Forget it. Go back to duty!" I had had no intention whatsoever of avoiding duty. I had simply delivered the doctor's message, as I had been instructed to do. I continued to receive night duty, but for some reason never felt any fear for my own safety—a factor most likely attributable to the folly of youth.

I do recall that while at the aid station, I occasionally saw jeeps coming in carrying GIs on stretchers. I didn't see any blood, nor did I hear any moaning. When I asked one of the medics what was wrong with those guys, he said, "Oh, they're just drunk. I guess they dug up too much of that good stuff."

. . . . .

An army in the field has all kinds of logistical problems, one of which is to arrange a sanitation system to take care of the soldiers' personal needs. The most obvious need was resolved by digging a latrine, sometimes called a slit trench. The dirt evacuated as the hole is dug is left at the side so that as each soldier finished using the latrine, he could shovel some of the dirt back into the hole. Sooner or later—usually sooner—the hole would be refilled, and it would be necessary to dig another latrine. A second problem, though, had no good solution. No one in the 5th Division—at least no one in the field—had enough water available to take a bath. The most that any soldier could do was to shave once in a while, but most often he could only splash his face a bit in the morning and wash his hands—sort of—before eating.

We had been given strict orders not to drink any water we found in the area because if we did, we would end up with the worst case of stomach cramps ever imagined. The drinking water that was provided for us was transported from the rear areas to an area near our position in large canvas bags. The bags were hung under a tripod and each had six or eight spouts at the bottom from which the soldiers filled their canteens. These spouts always reminded me of the teats on my cows back home, except that these were made of metal. The water was laced with litmus tablets to purify it, which gave it a distinctly noxious taste, but at least it was safe to drink. We were told that if we ever had to drink any of the local water, that we must purify it first with litmus tablets. Just as we had emergency bandage packs attached to our belts to hold gauze and penicillin powder, each of us also carried a vial of litmus tablets.

. . . . .

Anyone who has ever been a soldier knows that most of the time is spent in abject boredom. Of course there are also moments of high tension, but it is common for a soldier to spend many of those hours of boredom cleaning his personal gear—especially his rifle. I regarded my M-1 rifle as a personal friend. It was my duty and pleasure to ensure that the rifle was always in good operating condition. The cleaning mechanism was a metal thong with a hole to attach a string at one end and a hole at the other end to hold a small piece of cloth dampened with a few drops of oil to act as a wiper. The metal thong gave enough weight to the string so that when the rifle was held vertically, the thong would carry the string along with it through the barrel. Once the thong had been dropped down the barrel, the cloth would be inserted into its hole in the other end of thong and the whole apparatus would be pulled through the barrel.

Late one afternoon I was cleaning my M-1 and had pulled the string about halfway through the barrel when it broke. There was a rod designed especially to solve this problem, but I didn't have one, so the thong stayed lodged in the rifle barrel. I was trying to remove it when I was suddenly grabbed by an officer and ordered to accompany several other soldiers to seek out and capture reported German infiltrators. In spite of our diligent efforts, we didn't find any German soldiers—which was a good thing because if it had been necessary for me to fire my clogged rifle, the explosion would have blown up the rifle and probably me with it. I am quite grateful that we found no German infiltrators.

. . . . .

The soldiers of the 5th Division soon forgot about the noxious taste of our water, the discomfort of our foxholes and the difficulties of digging latrines, because as the sun began to rise on July 27, 1944, the 5th Division began to move forward.

For an individual soldier, especially a rifleman in the rear ranks, the horizon is somewhat limited. All that I could see as our unit began to move were the two infantry platoons and the heavy weapons platoon of my company leading the way, while my own platoon was held in reserve. My view was so limited that I could not actually see the other platoons, but I knew they were there, some 100 yards ahead moving forward through the hedgerow area. As each unit would encounter a hedgerow, the barrier would have to be negotiated somehow, usually through what appeared to be openings used by the French farmers to get from field to field. For the forward troops, this had to be accomplished under fire from the Jerries. The hedgerows, however, also provided useful shields to protect them from German resistance. At one point in the advance, as our squad approached a high embankment, we saw some of the guys from the forward platoon coming back in our direction, scurrying over and down the embankment in front of us. They were trying to avoid German artillery fire, which seemed to be following them murderously, and were shouting frantically to us that the Germans had zeroed in on them with their 88s (the German artillery rifle) and that we should take protected positions immediately. I remember seeing an American GI who was taking a young German prisoner to the rear for interrogation while the artillery shells were falling. He was trying to tell the German to take cover, but he did not speak German and his prisoner did not speak English. The only way he could communicate was to make hand motions signifying the incoming shells and an explosion. The German took note, understood, and they took cover together.

Our company commander was severely wounded in the lower abdomen during this artillery barrage. The medics placed him on a stretcher for evacuation to the rear and the company executive officer appointed four of us to take him back to the medical area. As we began to leave, I heard the medic exclaim, "Oh, my God, I think he's gone," to which the Executive Officer responded, "For heaven's sakes, someone cover his face." Although I had no love whatsoever lost for the Captain, I took off my shirt and placed it over his face. As we proceeded to evacuate him to the rear area medic station, I was wearing only my light field jacket on my upper body. When we reached the medical evacuation area, the captain, the stretcher and my shirt were all turned over to the medics. That was the last I ever saw of my shirt, although it may have been an even exchange, considering I wound up with the captain's Colt 45 automatic pistol. As we put the stretcher down I thought that I had always wanted one of those, so I just put it in my pocket. He wouldn't need it any more. The darned thing was a whole lot heavier in my pocket than I had expected.

On our way back to the company's forward position my companions and I got separated and all of a sudden I found myself alone. I continued in the direction I thought I should be going until I came across what appeared to be an alley with tall trees lining either side, forming a canopy overhead. The place looked familiar, so I started to run down the path between the trees, but as I neared the end of the alley I realized I had never been there before and turned to retrace my steps. At that point I realized that I was completely unprotected from any snipers that might have been left behind and I must admit I was more than a little scared. I got out of there as fast as I could and soon was able to find my way back to my platoon.

CHAPTER SIX
Capture

Upon return to our company area, our squad was almost immediately commandeered as part of an ammunition detail of 17 soldiers. We were again ordered to return to the rear area, this time to come back with ammunition bandoliers. Bandoliers were cloth belts containing clips of M-1 ammunition. They were hung over a soldier's shoulder and across his body and carried with him as he moved forward into battle, somewhat reminiscent of the Mexican bandits we used to see in old western movies.

As we were making our way to the ammo dump in the rear, I noticed the soldier in front of me carrying his rifle slung over his shoulder with its barrel hanging down. Suddenly it fired. We all jumped for cover, but it wasn't a sniper shooting at us. It was a guy looking for a ticket back to England—and then home—with only a wounded foot. Much to his consternation, no doubt, the round simply plowed up some dirt.

Once we reached the ammo dump, we each loaded six or seven bandoliers over our shoulders and began to trudge our way back to the delivery point. Suddenly we came under fire. We all dived for cover in a nearby ditch. We couldn't be sure, but the shots seemed to be coming from somewhere in front of us. I started firing my rifle in the general direction of this presumed enemy fire. The incoming fire stopped almost immediately and after a few minutes we felt it was safe to continue on our way with the ammo. When we reached our designated area behind a certain hedgerow, however, there were no Americans there. As the non-com in charge of the detail, a corporal, was trying to decide what we should do, enemy mortar shells started falling along the hedgerow just ahead of us. At the same time a heavy hail of small arms fire from rifles and machine guns began pelting the top of the hedgerow. The Germans had obviously played this game before. Just as we felt safe from the mortar shells because they were falling at the far end of the hedgerow, the shells started falling at the closer end and moving up toward us. We did the natural thing: We ran in the opposite direction, away from the exploding shells, but then the shells leap-frogged over us and headed us away from the other end. We were running in a crouched position to avoid the small arms fire. One of our guys was hit and began screaming. It may sound silly, but my reaction at the time was that because *I* didn't feel any pain at all, I couldn't understand why *he* was screaming.

As we were rushing toward the end of the hedgerow away from the last round of mortar shells, the mortars and the small arms fire suddenly ceased. I was in the lead when the firing stopped, so after a couple of minutes I began to straighten up. As I did, I looked up and there was a German soldier looking straight at me—and so was his MG-34 machine pistol. He and his companions were shouting in English, "Hands up, my boys. Hands up, my boys." There was nothing else to do; we could put our hands up or be shot. (I still wonder why he didn't shoot me.) We all dropped our rifles on the ground where we stood. Looking down, I thought I maybe I should have thrown mine farther away from me. So, what did I do? I reached down picked up my rifle and threw it a little farther away. The German soldier just looked at me, but I was sure he was thinking, "Go ahead, kid, just try it."

What had happened was that the American units that were supposed to be on our left and right flanks had pulled back. It was our bad luck that no one had thought to warn us and we were left exposed on both flanks. The Germans had surrounded us, coming around the forward hedgerow after having rattled us with the mortar shells.

We were herded through a break in a hedgerow about 100 yards forward to where the Germans had established a firing position facing the Americans. We were taken through another opening to an old stone building some 100 yards to their rear. On the way, I saw that we were being led through a line of German soldiers positioned on the rear side of a raised hedgerow. There were no trees or bushes on the top of this one; nevertheless, the Germans were using it as a protected position. These were infantry soldiers, each armed with a rifle and other small arms such as ground-mounted machine guns. I also noticed several German soldiers armed with strange-looking, barrel-shaped objects with balls at the bottom. These were probably some sort of bazooka, although I never knew for sure. The line of German soldiers extended for several hundred yards both to the right and to the left of the opening. It was a rather substantial German defensive position.

Upon reaching the building, German soldiers searched us, looking for guns, knives or anything else they considered dangerous to them. The truth was they were really looking for American Cigarettes. I can hear them now saying, "Cigarettes for the officers. Cigarettes for the officers." They got plenty of cigarettes, but I'd bet the officers never saw any of them. They dug into our backpacks as though it were Christmas morning and they had just looked under the tree for presents.

You will recall that I had removed my shirt earlier that day to cover the face of our deceased captain. My field jacket was a little too big and, without the shirt underneath, the sleeves partially covered my hands. This turned out to be a lucky break because the Germans did not see the watch that my parents had given me before I left for the army. If they had seen it, one of them surely would have taken it. Thus, I was able to keep my watch through not only the initial searching and interrogation, but all the way through my prisoner of war experience as well.

The Germans had us stand along the inside wall of the building while they searched us and our equipment. In addition to my gun, I had a hand-grenade in my right trouser pocket—and a scabbard and hunting knife strapped to my right leg and under my trousers—but before they got to me, a call came from their superior officer up at the firing line. He needed two prisoners sent up to him. Guess who was picked—a young Mexican guy and me. So as it turned out, the two of us were ordered to go back toward the German fire positions we had just come through, and the Germans never got around to searching me at all.

We did as we were told—having been told using gestures rather than words, since none of the Germans appeared to speak English and we didn't speak German. We ran back toward the German firing positions, but when we were about halfway there, a fierce hail of American small arms fire roared in our direction. As the Germans returned fire, some of the soldiers noticed me and my companion coming toward them through that hail of lead and frantically shouted and motioned to us to get down—in spite of the fact that they knew we were Americans. We did not respond and just kept going toward the German positions. I'm not sure how, but by some miracle, neither of us was hit. About the time we reached our destination, the firing subsided.

As we arrived at the German position, the German soldiers began pointing toward a small building that was off to the left, perhaps thirty to forty feet from the hedgerow the Germans were using for cover. We did not understand precisely what they wanted us to do, so we did nothing. About this time a German noncommissioned officer, or perhaps an officer, who had been watching this entire situation, approached us, removed his Luger from its holster, pointed it toward me and my companion and then toward the little building. We got the message.

We went the thirty or forty feet to the small building, which appeared to have been a

French barn or stable. When we entered, we saw what it was that we were being told to do. A wounded German soldier was lying on the floor with a gaping hole in his left shoulder. The wound appeared to be quite severe, with flesh oozing out from the damaged area. We then understood that we were being told to carry this soldier back toward the rear of the German lines for medical attention. About this time an American mortar shell struck the far side of the building and set the whole thing on fire. There was a considerable amount of straw piled up inside the building that we knew was sure to go up in flames at any moment. Evidently, the German soldier wasn't wounded quite as badly as the other Germans had feared, because once the fire started, he got up from the floor and ran like hell out of the building and toward the rear of the German lines, with us following close behind. By that time, the other American prisoners had been brought forward and we rejoined the group and proceeded to the right, behind the German defensive positions and away from the battle area.

I remember quite vividly the lay of the land in this particular spot behind the defensive German positions. The general location was to the east of St. Lo, somewhere between St. Lo and Caen. As I turned my back to the German positions and looked toward the south, I saw a wide expanse of green pasture that I knew was excellent for grazing cattle. To the south of this pasture was a great, blue lake, which I knew must have held thousands of bass or catfish, or you name it. To the far left was a slight rise, a small hill covered with trees. The view was a beautiful sight for a country boy from Putnam County, Georgia. As we were being marched away I looked back and saw one of our fighter-bombers coming in low over the lake. As I watched, I saw him drop two bombs.

CHAPTER SEVEN
Journey to Adorf - *Du Juden?*

Our band of prisoners was escorted for some distance behind the German firing lines, turning south through a heavily wooded area to a small country roadway. It was around noon when we reached the road and we continued south along it for most of the remainder of the afternoon, probably until dark. Eventually we arrived at what appeared to be a small French farm and were taken to one of the outbuildings. The building was about twenty feet square with a door and several windows and looked like it had probably been used as a stable sometime in the past. We were ordered to go in and sit down and the Germans closed and locked the door.

In a few minutes one of the German privates opened the door, pointed to me and another guy and said, "Come, come." When we were outside he slammed the door and locked it again. Motioning us to go ahead of him, he guided us by pointing his rifle in the direction he wanted us to take. We did as we were told. We went to what had been the farm storage shed, where we found a roll of barbed wire. We pushed a stick through the center of the roll and carried the wire back the stable. When we got there he made us crisscross the windows and nearly all of the door with the wire and use a hammer he had brought with him to nail it in place. When we finished, he reached through the wire, unlocked the door and told us to go in under the wire, which, of course, we did. After the door was shut and locked, we heard him nailing more barbed wire onto it. We were later given food of some sort by someone handing it to us through the barbed wire.

We spent the night in this building. It must have been a fairly comfortable prison cell because I have no adverse memories of that particular evening. Actually, it had been one hell of a long day and a hell of a lot had happened to us, so I guess we all just collapsed. During the night I prudently "lost" the hand grenade and hunting knife in a dark corner. They had bedeviled me for the past twelve hours because I knew that if the Germans found them on me, there is no telling what they might do. I will say, however, that since we were now away from the fighting and were, in effect, noncombatants, the German soldiers were downright friendly. I guess we were all just boys, each curious about the other. This was the 28th of July, 1944, and I had turned twenty just thirteen days before. When the sun came up we heard banging as the German private tried to knock the wire off the door. When he finally succeeded, we were ordered out of our stable and given some coffee, marmalade and bread.

As we were finishing our breakfast, some of the Germans gathered around us—not in a hostile way, but to try to talk to us. It turned out these were paratroopers who no longer had any airplanes. The German soldiers showed absolutely no animosity toward us and there was none from the Americans toward the Germans. The atmosphere was not tense at all and we guys, both the Germans and the Americans, tried to communicate with one another as best we could. One German soldier came up to me and pulled from his wallet a picture of several German paratroopers standing or kneeling by the side of a German aircraft. He was telling me that this was a picture of his squad and I could tell how proud he was of them. Another German came over and pulled out a knife similar to an American switchblade from his pocket. It wasn't an aggressive move; he simply wanted to show me his knife and how proud he was that he had it.

Several of the German paratroopers asked us, "Chicago? You from Chicago? You Chicago gangster?" Then they would hold their hands close together and point as if holding a machine gun and say, "Rat-a-tat-tat, Rat-a-tat-tat." After a few minutes of this type of banter, the Germans motioned us to form lines and move out, walking south along the roadway. We walked for several hours over fairly level countryside, stopping around noon at a French house close by the road.

By this time we had been joined by a couple of other groups of American, British and Canadian prisoners. We had all been walking at a brisk pace and were happy to stop. Two or three of the GIs were from Air Force bomber crews who had bailed out and been captured. These poor fellows were still wearing their flight suits, or parts of them. At the least they were wearing fleece-lined boots, and they were hot.

We were supposed to be fed, so the Germans required the French family who lived in the house to prepare and serve food for us. We were told to wait outside in front of the house under the watchful eye of a couple of the German soldiers while the noncom went inside to make the arrangements. The French family was as friendly to us as the situation would permit. The food was simple, but it was all they had. While we were eating, standing up and milling around, I noticed one of the family's daughters—I guessed she was about fifteen years old—giving one of the guys the eye. When she got his attention she was standing next to a stairway leading down to somewhere. In her futile attempt to get him to ease down the stairway and make his escape she had put herself and her family in imminent danger. The stupid fellow couldn't understand what she was doing; he thought she wanted his body, or so he said later.

After spending a short time at the French house, the German guards motioned to us again to form our lines on either side of the road and continue going in a southerly direction. We had learned a couple of German words: *los*, which means hurry in English, and *mach schnel*—which literally means "make fast", but we heard it as "Hurry up!" or "Make it quick!" More and more Americans and other allied POWs were added to our ranks as we walked, again some wearing the fleece-lined boots issued to American bomber crews. Those boots had to be very uncomfortable in the July heat.

About midafternoon we arrived at a small village and were herded into the town square where we joined still other American prisoners of war. We were all required to remain standing or sitting on the ground in the center of the square. There were many French civilians watching from the other side the surrounding streets. From time to time one of them would run across the street and hand something to one of the POWs. The Germans, of course, saw this and shooed them back across the street. The soldiers were not particularly rough in restraining the civilians. In fact, they were rather lenient in permitting them to hand things to the Americans.

It turned out that what they were giving the Americans—and the Germans obviously knew this—were raw eggs and bread, and even an occasional cup of Benedictine. I could not enjoy the raw eggs as some of the GIs did. They would punch a little hole in each end of the egg and then suck out the contents and gain some nourishment. I was not ready to eat an egg in this fashion—no matter how hungry I was.

After spending about an hour or two, maybe more, in the central square of this small village, the entire POW contingent was herded onto German army trucks and transported eastward toward Rheims, France. Sometime during this truck trip—and my calculations tell me that this had to be at least a five- to six-hour trip—the we stopped near a railroad junction where we could see several railroad cars packed with provisions. The cars appeared to have been backed off the main track into a forested area where they would be protected by the large trees from being seen from the air. The Germans ordered us off the trucks and had us unload large sacks—like the feed sacks I had known on the farm in Eatonton—from the boxcars. We placed the sacks on the ground beside the cars for someone else to cart away. The sacks themselves were light but bulky, and appeared to contain foodstuffs of some sort.

Sometime during this offloading operation, the German guards started shouting, "Flee-ah, flee-ah, flee-ah!" and herding us up under the train cars and out of sight. They were actually yelling "Flier, flier, flier!" because they had heard approaching aircraft and feared that an American or British pilot would be attracted by the activity and sustain an air-raid at the offloading point. Evidently we were not seen and the planes just flew over our location, heading south somewhere else. After this incident, we finished the offloading operation, were ordered back onto the trucks, and continued heading east towards Rheims. We wouldn't have to spend the night on the road, since Rheims was only a short distance away.

It was late in the afternoon when the two German trucks in which we were traveling reached a rail marshaling yard in Rheims, France. There we saw a long train of European boxcars, familiarly referred to as "40 or 8s"—a term left over from World War I that meant the cars could hold either 40 men or eight horses. We, along with other Allied prisoners from other locations, were loaded aboard these boxcars—40 men to each car.

It was crowded and hot in the boxcar, with barely enough room to sit down and certainly not enough to lie down. Once the boxcars were loaded, they were closed, leaving us inside in total darkness. There were no windows, so we could not see outside of the car and it was therefore impossible for us to tell whether it was daytime or nighttime. We didn't know it then, but we were on our way to a large transit camp at Meuleberg, Germany.

At one point during the transit from Rheims, the train stopped and all of the prisoners were permitted to disembark and relieve ourselves on the tracks beside the train. This was the first time I had participated in a public pee. Afterwards we were herded back into the cars, the train resumed its journey, and darkness again pervaded the interior of the cars.

Along the way I had become friends with a great big guy from Texas. He mentioned to me that although he didn't smoke, he had several packs of Lucky Strikes, and if I wanted them I was welcome to them. Well, I did smoke, so I accepted his offer and smoked one after another. After a while one of the guys sitting next to me commented that I sure was smoking a lot. He also said those cigarettes were worth more than their weight in gold. With that my former friend took back every one I hadn't smoked.

It was again late in the afternoon when the trainload of POWs arrived in Meuleberg, a marshaling point for American, British, Canadian, Australian and New Zealander prisoners from all parts of the French front. Here there were open, barn-like buildings without walls, but with straw mats on the floor to serve as beds. The entire area was fenced in, and all the POWs from the various locations along the Western Front were herded into these buildings. Hundreds and hundreds of POWs passed through Meuleberg during the few days I was there before we were sent to the next prison camp. The Germans were very careful to ensure that groups of soldiers who had come in together were split up before boarding the trains from Meuleberg to Merseberg, which would be our next stop. Hence I found myself totally separated from the 17 soldiers with whom I had been captured. I did not see any of them for the remainder of my time in Germany, nor have I seen them since. The train ride to Merseburg, Germany, again on the "40 or 8s," took no more than one day and was uneventful. But once we arrived, things began to happen.

The transition camp at Merseburg was an enormous compound with many large buildings similar to the ones at Meuleberg. These buildings did have exterior walls, but had no interior walls. Inside there were long rows of straw mats laid out on the floor, with aisles separating the rows. They were just huge structures where hundreds of American, British, Canadian, Australian and New Zealander soldiers could be housed.

As the train pulled into the compound, the prisoners were required to disembark and to stand in groups in a vast field in the middle of which was a small table where two German officers were seated. We were separated from the table by at least one hundred yards and there were several buildings about another hundred yards beyond it, making it impossible for anyone to hear what was being said during the interrogations. One by one the POWs were required to go to the table and speak to the German officers, one of whom spoke flawless English with a distinctly British accent.

As I approached the table, the English-speaking officer looked at me and said, "Your papers, please." I had no official papers, but I removed my wallet and put it on the table along with everything else in my pockets. The German looked at the contents of the wallet, but said nothing for a little while. After standing there for some time while nothing was happening I said to him, "If you are through with it, I'll put all this trash back in my pocket." The officer looked up at me with a scowl in his voice and said, "Don't be cheeky. Pick that trash up and go to that building," pointing to the building where, as I soon discovered, the showers were located. The other officer did not utter a word the whole time I was standing there. He just looked at me. After retrieving my meager belongings, I went to the building he had indicated. There I was told to take off my clothes and take a shower.

That took care of my filthy clothing. I never saw any of it again.

After the shower, I joined a long line of other POWs who were being herded, totally nude, into what appeared to be a dispensary where we were each given a brief medical examination and some sort of inoculation. During the examination a German medic looked at me and, noticing my circumcision, asked, "*Du Jude?*" (I have since learned that by using *du*, the familiar form of "you," he was not only questioning my religious status, but was speaking to me in a derisive tone. In this context, *du* is patently inappropriate; only the more formal form, *sie*, would have been proper.) I responded with a grunt. Finally, the entire group filed through a supply area where we were issued prison clothes, which I think must have been clothing left behind by other POWs on their way to take their showers. At this point we were given forms to fill out asking primarily for name, rank, home address, next of kin and religious preference. I filled in the form correctly—except for the last question. I wrote "Protestant."

The compound at Merseburg was divided into two sections separated by a tall wire fence with coiled barbed wire on the top. One section held Americans, British, French, Australians, New Zealanders and Canadians. The other was reserved entirely for Russian prisoners. The German guards treated the Russian prisoners very harshly; in fact, they were downright mean. It was not uncommon to look through the barbed wire fence and see a German soldier hitting a Russian with the butt of his rifle simply because the Russian hadn't moved fast enough. We were treated in a more civil manner on our side of the fence.

The food we had was mostly bread and cheese. The bread came in wedges, each probably weighing close to a quarter of a kilogram, about half a pound. We would cut the bread into thin slices and place them out in the hot sun where they would soon dry out and become much like toast. This "toast" was frequently accompanied by orange marmalade or various types of cheeses that the Germans would issue to us. The cheeses came in a variety of forms and sizes and in different types of packages. On one occasion the cheese arrived in tin cans about the size of the small cans of salmon you could find in your local supermarket. The cans were puffed out on both ends, which today would be a clear signal not to eat the contents, but some of us gleefully opened the cans anyway. We were greeted with a loud hiss and a spray of strong odor. I thought that was great and ate the cheese—probably Limburger, although I am not sure—without another thought. Many of the prisoners would not eat it, so some of the others—including Frederick Scheer—got extra rations.

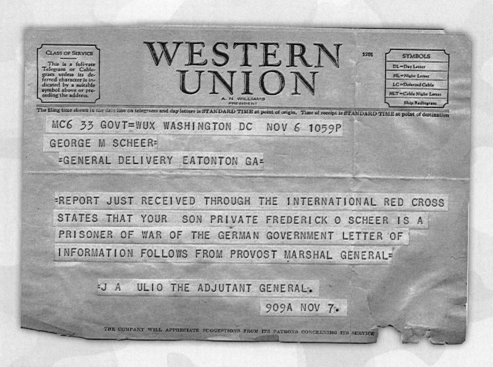

The filing time shown in the date line on telegrams and day letters is STANDARD TIME at point of origin. Time of receipt is STANDARD TIME at point of destination

MC6 33 GOVT=WUX WASHINGTON DC   NOV 6 1059P

GEORGE M SCHEER=

=GENERAL DELIVERY EATONTON GA=

=REPORT JUST RECEIVED THROUGH THE INTERNATIONAL RED CROSS
STATES THAT YOUR SON PRIVATE FREDERICK O SCHEER IS A
PRISONER OF WAR OF THE GERMAN GOVERNMENT LETTER OF
INFORMATION FOLLOWS FROM PROVOST MARSHAL GENERAL=

=J A ULIO THE ADJUTANT GENERAL.

909A NOV 7.

THE COMPANY WILL APPRECIATE SUGGESTIONS FROM ITS PATRONS CONCERNING ITS SERVICE

My Dad liked all sorts of strange foods including strong, foul-smelling cheeses, and had taught me to love them, too.

It was at Merseburg that I had my first contact with the organizational structures fashioned by POWs in the camps. These systems were condoned, maybe even fostered, by the German authorities because they helped them manage the prisoners and made the administration of the camp much easier. Nevertheless, the prisoners regarded those who took part in these loose structures as friends, not as lackeys of the Germans, because the arrangement existed solely to make the prison life easier on the prisoners themselves.

During my short stay—only four or five days—at Merseburg, several members of that organizational structure approached me to help me acclimate myself to prison conditions. They also provided me with writing materials so that I could write a letter home. I told them I wanted to write to Nelly, but they very wisely encouraged me to write to my folks instead. Because I would only be permitted to write one letter at that time, they strongly advised that I should write to my mother and father in Eatonton so that they would know I was safe. I did as I was told.

When I got home I heard the story of how my folks found out that my letter had arrived. To start with, a small town like Eatonton is like a big family—everyone knows what is happening in everybody else's life. When Mr. Nelson, the Eatonton postmaster, sorted the mail and came across my letter, he screamed and ran out of the post office without even taking off his apron. He didn't want to make a phone call because he would have had to explain to the telephone operator why he was so excited and that would have taken too much time. Instead he ran the three blocks to Dad's store. I can almost hear him as he ran up the street waving the envelope in the air and shouting, "George and Florence got a letter from Frederick!" When he got to the store, he ran in hollering "George, George, look what I got!!"

Frederick Scheer Is War Prisoner

EATONTON, Nov. 1—Mr. and Mrs. George M. Scheer today received a letter from their son, Frederick Scheer, who was reported several months ago a German war prisoner.

The letter which is the first received since being a war prisoner, was dated September 1 and arrived almost two months from date of writing. He reports being well taken care of and receiving a box each week from the Red Cross.

Daddy almost collapsed when he opened the letter. By this time there was a crowd forming in the front of the store. Our family friend and Dad's store manager Lillie Weems—everyone called her Miss Lillie—was telling everyone what had happened as Daddy ran out of the store and headed for the high school where Mother was helping my younger sister's class get ready for some sort of function taking place that night. Everyone was overjoyed to hear that I was safe.

During my stay at Merseburg, I somehow obtained a piece of chewy candy and as I was eating it, lost one of my fillings. I knew it was necessary to have it replaced, but who would have thought that in a place like this you could just go visit your friendly family dentist? You're right; you couldn't. But my tooth got repaired, nonetheless.

I was told there was a dentist who had set up practice in a particular area of the exercise yard. Well, stranger things have happened, so I headed for the exercise yard, wondering whether the female dental assistant would look like an old bag or a GI's dream. You guessed it; she was neither. Picture if you will a vast prison yard with hundreds of prisoners-of-war milling to and fro. In the middle of the yard was a single straight chair—with arms so you could brace yourself when the pain began to test your manhood. Standing beside the chair was a strange cable-and-pulley device that turned out to be a mechanism to run the dentist's drill. There was no electricity, so the drill had to be powered by hand. The so-called dental assistant was a great big guy who had been a truck driver in his pre-army life. He would turn a wheel that was about two feet in diameter and a series of cables and pulleys made the drill turn. Needless to say, there was no Novocain or any other type of medication, but when the dentist told me to open my mouth, I did. As the dental assistant turned the wheel, the drill started to buzz and the dentist started to prepare the tooth for the filling saying, "Hold on this is going to hurt." He had not even started and he was already telling me it was going to hurt. But it didn't hurt because I had already had a root canal on that tooth and hence felt no pain at all. They couldn't believe that I could be such a man. There was also no water there, so I couldn't rinse out my mouth. Believe it or not, I still have that filling.

One traumatic incident occurred toward the end of my time at Merseburg. On this particular day, about eighty of us were called out for transport to a work camp at Adorf, Germany. The German officer in charge announced to these eighty soldiers that it was against German federal law for a member of the Jewish faith to work in Germany and that since we were being transported to a work camp, it was necessary to identify and remove from the group all members of the Jewish faith. He then called out several names that he must have thought sounded Jewish and those individuals were required to leave the group. He then said, "Are there any other members of the Jewish faith in this group?" Several of the Americans stepped forward and were removed, but I kept my counsel, deciding that it was in my best interest to stay with the group and head for the work camp. The POWs who had been removed were replaced by others to complete the required number.[4] Although there was a mixture of American, British, Canadian, Australian and New Zealanders in this tremendous camp, only American prisoners were included in this group of eighty men. It is my guess that the Germans did not want any experienced hands in our group. Many of the members of the other forces had been captured in North Africa and had been POWs for over three years. Those guys knew the ropes.

The eighty men boarded the "40 or 8" train cars and headed for Adorf, Germany, and Stalag "IV-F". This was to be my permanent residence until close to the end of the war in Europe.

---

1   The Germans routinely segregated Jewish POWs, sending many to labor and concentration camps where they were routinely starved and otherwise mistreated. The locations of these camps seldom appear on WWII maps. (Bard, Mitchell. Jewish POWs in a Nazi Concentration Camp. n.d. http://www.mitchellbard.com/articles/pows.html. Accessed November 29, 2010)

This is my POW tag issued at Merseburg.
My POW number was acht (8) drei (3)
sechs (6) neun (9) zwei (2).

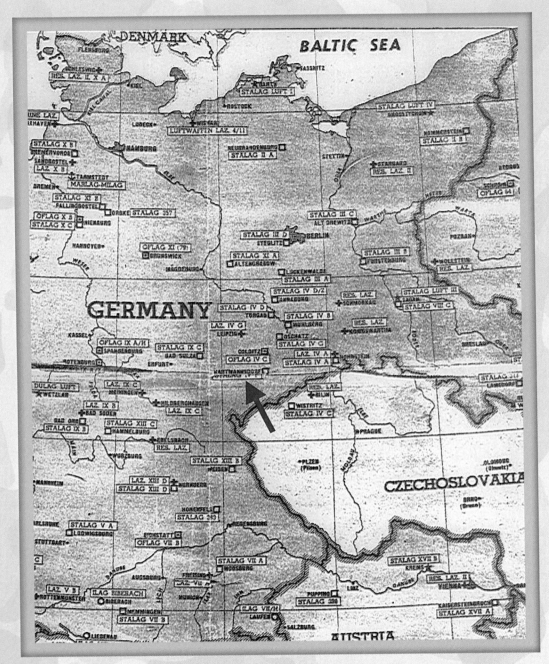

Location of Stalag IV-F.

CHAPTER EIGHT
Stalag IV-F - Adorf, Germany

The Camp

Adorf, Germany, was a major rail center located in the Bavarian countryside of eastern Germany about sixty kilometers east of the city of Plauen and another sixty kilometers west of the Czech border. Our group arrived at Stalag IV-F in the early morning hours. The sun was shining, but not brightly, through the partial overcast.

The camp was located adjacent to the railroad tracks and was used as a work camp to house prisoners assigned to work in and about the railroad yard and along the railroad tracks leading to and from the area. It was quite small, consisting only of a fenced compound containing one large wooden, single-story, U-shaped building It is possible that it had once been a railway workers' camp, but no one really knows.

The building itself contained four sections, each housing twenty prisoners. A section consisted of a living area and a sleeping area. Each room was equipped with an old coal-fired potbellied stove. The latrines and wash basins were located in the middle of the building. There were no showers or bathing facilities, but the prisoners were occasionally permitted to use the showers in the nearby roundhouse.

The living area was not like any living room to which I was accustomed. Actually it was a day room with tables placed along the walls. Each POW had his own place at a table, as well as shelf space above the table where he could store his personal belongings, which usually amounted to any food he might have saved and any other possession he had acquired but did not want to carry in his pocket when he went out to work. It was not necessary to have any closet or hanging space because we didn't have anything to hang up. The only clothing we had was a single shirt, a pair of pants (and these were often so dirty they could stand up by themselves), one set of underwear, a pair of socks, and an overcoat. The overcoat had a large orange triangle in the middle of the back about shoulder high. Frequently the coat sported a nice round bullet hole either between the shoulder blades or in the chest area. The triangle on the back of the coat made a great target if the person wearing it decided to run away.

The soles of our shoes eventually wore thin and we started to put pieces of newspaper in them to help keep out the cold. By this time our socks weren't much good, anyway. When the weather turned cold, our coats became added cover on our bunks at night. These items constituted all of a POW's worldly possessions and they meant everything to him. Think about it: All that we owned was carried, either on our backs or in our pockets, or was kept in a little pasteboard box on a shelf. These articles were all in the world we could claim as our own.

We were permitted the freedom of the entire compound during the evening hours, from the time we returned from our work details until 9:00 p.m., and all day on Sunday. At 9:00 p.m. the German guards required us to undress, which meant stripping down to our underwear, overcoat and shoes (no socks). Then we would go into our sleeping room where we would be locked in for the night.

The sleeping area was furnished with double-decker bunks. Each bunk came equipped with a straw mattress, accompanied by an ample supply of bed bugs. In the corner of the room was a large wooden box that held coal briquettes to fire the stove. There were never enough briquettes to keep the room at any comfortable temperature when the weather turned cold. When we had arrived at Stalag IV-F in September, the weather was still summery. The briquettes provided by the Germans were primarily used to heat water for the wash basins in the latrine, but the supply of was always insufficient for making hot water. When we complained about the lack of hot water, the Germans said there were not enough briquettes to use for that purpose and that "*Krieg ist krieg.*" (War is war.) That was the answer to any such request. We noted that the guards must have had enough hot water because none of them ever looked like he needed a shave. As far as heating the rooms when the weather was cold, we would just have to make out as best we could. And we did.

The compound consisted solely of the U-shaped building and one other small structure located in the opening of the U. There was a gate adjacent to this building separating the compound from the outside world. This opening led to a path along the edge of the coaling station, which was part of the roundhouse complex and was used by the public. The building was occupied by the camp commander—a German corporal with a very high-pitched voice. He was not a large man, but his peaked uniform cap and starched green uniform made him look like someone to be reckoned with. Like many German men, he sported a little black "Hitler mustache," of which he was very proud. The entire camp administration consisted principally of older German soldiers known as *volkssturm*.[5] Including the corporal, there were probably six or eight of these *volkssturm* members assigned to the camp. The relationship between the prison authorities and the POWs was, shall we say, amiable.

The area in the center of the "U" was flat like a mini-parade ground. We were required to assemble there every day before departing for and upon returning from our work details. The corporal would come out of his office, look us over and, if he did not see anything unusual, we would be sent off to work or dismissed. If, on the other hand, he thought we were trying to put something over on him, he would stand there and rant and rave in German—several octaves above normal. We couldn't understand anything he said, but we got the message. Eventually he would get tired and dismiss us so he could go back to his office and we could go on to work or to our barracks. It was just like being in the army—the German army. In reality, those of us living in the compound were a part of the German railroad system: We were being leased to the railroad company by whatever German government department owned us. Our status was the same as that of any piece of leased equipment or work animal and as such our camp was right beside the railroad switch track.

The rail center was quite a bustling place. It was a major switching center and the yard held a huge number of freight cars that were continually being moved up and down the switch track.[6] The roundhouse always had a number of steam engines, each with its nose sticking in through one of the bays, and a great many more waiting their turns to enter. A coaling station was used to replenish the coal supply as the engines passed through.

Each POW was assigned to a special work detail. About four or five were assigned to the roundhouse, where they worked as mechanic's helpers. They must have worked as grease monkeys, judging by what they looked like when they returned to camp in the evening. Another four or five men were assigned to the coaling station. These guys spent most of their days shoveling small piles of scrap coal into larger piles. Four more were sent to work in a factory. I never found out what they did, just that they came home every night. They were

---

1   *Volkssturm*, literally "folk storm," was a German national militia created in the last months of World War II as a result of the total mobilization of men from 16 to 60 years of age.

2   The Germans switched the rail cars by first backing a long line of cars onto the switching track, which ran up a hill between the major yard and the prison compound. Then they locked the brakes on all the cars in the line and disconnected and removed the engine. When they released the brakes on the each car in turn, gravity would take over and the car would roll down the hill, picking up enough momentum to be switched from one track to another as it reached the bottom of the hill.

the lucky ones, though, because they worked inside a factory building during the winter. The rest of us were divided into two groups, each of which was assigned to one of two section labor gangs. In railroad parlance, section labor refers to repairing and maintaining the tracks. I was usually assigned to one of those work crews, although occasionally I worked in the coaling yard.

At the outset of our incarceration in Stalag IV-F, we were each issued a metal bowl and a metal cup, both brown on the outside and blue on the inside, and a spoon. The bowl would hold about four cups of whatever food we were given. The standard daily ration started in the morning with a cup of ersatz coffee and quarter kilo of dark German bread. I think the coffee was made from barley or some other grain. In the evening we received a bowl of small boiled potatoes and another cup of ersatz coffee. For protein we each received a weekly patty of a concoction we affectionately called "bloodwurst". We never quite determined what this bloodwurst actually was, but it supplied protein derived from some kind of animal. Maybe it was just the worst of the worst. You would be surprised at the joy we felt at receiving that bowl of little potatoes. Some of the guys just ate them as they were, but others, including me, often stopped to peel them. As time went by, the boiled potatoes became potato soup and the potato soup became thinner and thinner and thinner. Eventually, it was frequently replaced by a gruel made from some sort of a grain mixture cooked in water. I could not abide the stuff and threw it in the latrine. Along about this same time, the bloodwurst disappeared entirely and no other form of protein was provided.

There was, however, some additional food available to us. This took two forms: Red Cross food packages and whatever we could find by foraging. The Red Cross packages arrived once a month and each package had to be shared by two POW's. Each package contained a large can of powdered milk, some large round wafers, about half a pound of coffee, a bar of soap, two packs of cigarettes, some powdered eggs, a can of spam, and some sweet cookies. On the black market, the soap, coffee and cigarettes were equivalent to the gold at Ft. Knox.

So it was that my compadres and I—a group of about 80 Americans—settled in for the long stay at Stalag IV-F. The stay was to last approximately nine months until late in April of 1945.

American Ingenuity

The pot-bellied stoves in our barracks were used not only for warmth, but they had a flat circular top that made an excellent surface for cooking. We prisoners, showing that famous American ingenuity, learned to soak the wafers in the powdered milk overnight on Saturday night and cook them as pancakes in the morning for a Sunday treat. I considered these pancakes quite a delicacy. (I tried this when I returned home, but they weren't the same at all. In fact, when made with soda crackers—saltine crackers without the salt—they were awful.) Sunday morning was a time to relax and enjoy the few little pleasures that we had.

The standard prison diet was also augmented by items we came across while on work detail. Occasionally, a prisoner would come back with a head of cabbage. He ate well that night. I once helped myself to several rutabagas from a German field. I had never liked rutabagas, but I took them back to the barracks anyway because it was the thing to do. On Sunday morning, hoping for a treat, I peeled them, cut them into small pieces and put them on the stove to boil. I salted them and watched them boil, anticipating how great this meal was going to be. When I thought they were ready, I tried them and discovered that, no matter how hungry I was, I still couldn't stand rutabagas. I gave the whole mess away.

I remember vividly a redheaded fellow named Olsen from North Dakota whose table space in the day room was adjacent to mine. I remember him so clearly because we had become close friends and I could not help but notice that he seemed to grow more emaciated by the day, to the point that at the end of our stay at Stalag IV-F, his ribs and shoulder bones were sharply visible. He was an unhealthy sight to see and I often wonder what became of him.

One Sunday morning I found one of the guys standing at our pot-bellied stove and—I couldn't believe my eyes—frying two eggs! He had acquired them somehow the day before—most likely stolen from a farmer's henhouse. While he was standing there with spoon in hand to turn them over, one of the German guards wandered through. With some amazement the guard asked where he had gotten the eggs. My friend, without hesitation, replied, "Oh, you know the powdered eggs in the Red Cross packets? Well I simply reconstituted them." The German guard just shook his head in amazement and walked away.

One of the standard techniques adopted by the POW's to aid in our foraging activities was to wear our overcoats as capes, which left our hands and arms free to conceal and carry our finds underneath. We also discovered that it was useful to tie our pant legs at the bottom near our ankles so that we could store and carry things there as well. After we had been at Stalag IV-F for a while, the corporal discontinued his inspections, unless one of the guards asked to do one.

When the weather began to grow cold, we needed more heat in our quarters. The Germans gave us no additional coal briquettes, so we found a way to solve the problem ourselves. Our work details went out each morning, walking on the path at the edge of the coaling station. As we walked single file in a long line with one guard in front and one in the back, we noticed that there were small piles of coal alongside the path. When we returned to camp in the evening we walked past those same piles of coal. Wearing his coat in the proper POW style, a guy could just slump down a bit, grab a lump of coal and secure it under his coat. The guards would yell at him to put the coal back, but when he didn't, the guards did nothing. Then after a few trips, it was clear that nothing would happen when the guards hollered, so more and more of our guys picked up coal, and eventually the guards stopped hollering altogether. At that point, any of us who had a free hand would grab coal. At least most of us did; there were always some guys who were too scared to do anything.

In the early fall the coal boxes in our rooms would have just enough briquettes in them to cover the bottom of the box. We only needed the coal for cooking, so we didn't use very much. We weren't very good at POW survival at that point, but as the weather got cold and we became more experienced, the boxes would be full to overflowing after we unloaded our purloined supply. We used some of the coal overnight, but in the morning the boxes would still be nearly full. When we returned from our work details in the evening however, the coal boxes would be less than half full. The fact was that the guards found our inventiveness to their advantage—they didn't have enough briquettes to keep their quarters warm either. It was obvious that we were stealing coal from them and then they were turning right around and stealing it back from us! The system was keeping everyone happy—and warm. It wasn't long before the German guards didn't even bother to look the other way when we picked up the coal. After all, we were saving them the trouble.

On Sunday mornings one of the guards would select a detail of six or eight POWs to take the hand-drawn wagon into the railroad commissary for the Sunday food rations. On one particular Sunday, the guard chose several other guys and me to make the trip. On these excursions the guard was usually somewhat relaxed and did not watch us as closely as he would have if he were being supervised. While we were waiting for our rations to be prepared and loaded onto the wagon, a buddy and I walked away from the group and stepped down into a storage cellar, where we discovered a whole cache of carrots. I promptly stuffed as many as I could into my pant leg. When we had sampled a couple of fresh ones for ourselves, we decided that we had been away long enough and headed back to rejoin the others. They had just finished loading the wagon and were ready to return to the camp, so the guard had started to look around for us. When he saw us come up from the cellar, he must have noticed something about me that was a little unusual. He checked me over, found my stash, made me return the carrots to the bin from which I had taken them, and we returned to camp. He didn't raise any hell about what I had done, but thereafter I was known affectionately by my friends as "Carrots."

On work days we would leave the barracks early in the morning and march single file toward the railroad depot, one German guard in front of the column and another at the rear. We would then board a train, a standard coach car, and be transported to our work site, usually fifty or sixty kilometers from the camp. Often the route took us through the mountains, where the scenery was beautiful, especially when the weather was cold and the mountains had snow on them. Sometimes during these transits we encountered electricians, usually Czechoslovakian, who worked on the electrical systems and the communication lines of the railroad. We referred to them as Czech linemen. During the trip back from the work site to the camp, it was not unusual for certain black market trading to take place between the Czech linemen and the American POWs. There was a German law against trading on the Black Market, but we considered ourselves above the German laws—or to put it another way, we didn't give a damn about the German laws. We felt that any little trick we could play on the Germans was a boost to the American war effort. For some of us this was a great game. Activities like these made us feel superior and provided a mental defense against German attempts to demoralize us.

The Czech linemen evidently had an arrangement with German bakers in the area that allowed them to procure loaves of bread in some quantity. These round loaves of German bread, about 12 to 14 inches in diameter and about three to four inches thick, were simply delicious—and the linemen had them in considerable abundance. The coffee, soap and cigarettes that we received in the Red Cross packages were like bars of yellow gold to these guys. One pack of Lucky Strikes or one bar of American soap or a half-pound package of coffee would buy one loaf of bread. Sometimes the Red Cross packages included a veritable pot of gold—a chocolate bar. A chocolate bar was as good as, if not better than, a pair of nylons—which we couldn't get anyway. A chocolate bar could get you anything you wanted.

The only problem with this system was that many of the POWs were afraid to trade. They thought something awful would happen to them if they were caught. There were some American POWs, however, who were willing to take the risk—and Frederick Oscar Scheer was one of them. Frankly, I didn't think there was much risk. What could they do to us, other than shoot us? I thought they needed the slave labor too much for that, so I joined the game. The risk was made worthwhile by the fact that whenever a POW exchanged a pack of cigarettes for a loaf of bread, he received a replacement pack plus a commission of two additional cigarettes. You may not think two cigarettes are worth much, but in that environment—and I don't mean the bad air—they were as good as pure gold. The commissions added up quickly, and soon the American trader had another pack of cigarettes, which he could then trade for another loaf of bread. Let's face it, most of us smoked, so the commissions provided a great incentive to get into the business. It was all a part of our survival.

When we returned to the train station at Adorf, we once again formed a single file line with a German guard in the front and another in the rear and marched back to the barracks with the bread held carefully in our arms and concealed under our overcoats. As we passed the coaling station, anyone with a free hand picked up lumps of coal and concealed them under his overcoat as well.

Most of the time, the bread and the coal went either unnoticed or ignored by the German guards. On one particular evening though, one of the guards decided not to ignore the loaves of bread that he probably knew beforehand would be concealed beneath a certain POW's overcoat. The POW was a real smart ass, or thought he was, and had smarted off at him early that morning while we were on the way to the work site, so now the guard had it in for him. He challenged the POW and made him pull the loaf of bread from beneath his coat. He made all of us stand in line while he turned the POW and his loaf of bread over to the camp commander. The corporal proceeded to upbraid the POW, yelling at him: "This is wrong, what you are doing, and now you must share this loaf of bread with your comrades." When he had finished his loud, high-pitched, raving speech he started to walk through the barracks with the loaf of bread under his left arm and a long butcher knife in his right hand. He required every POW to sit in his respective place in the day room. Then, starting at one end of the barracks with the offending POW being marched ahead of him by another guard, he walked through the entire barracks, slicing off a piece of bread for each POW as he went, until the bread was gone. With each slice he repeated to the offender, "You must share with your comrades." Little did he realize that a short distance behind him, another POW was picking up each slice as he went. In the end, the entire loaf was returned to its original owner. Even better: now it was sliced. There was no additional punishment meted out to the guy and he became an avid bread trader.

The Work

I spent most of my time at the prison camp working in one of the section crews. Each morning we would leave the camp, walk to the railroad station, board a train, travel fifty or sixty kilometers, and spend the day repairing the railroad tracks. We were generally issued two tools: a pitchfork and an instrument that resembled an American pickaxe. The back end of the pickaxe was shaped something like a club and its wooden handle was approximately three feet long. We dubbed it the "hocker"—which sounded to us like what the Germans were calling it. The pitchfork, was just like the ones we used on the farm back home. We used them here to move aggregate and stone about from place to place. When we had to move a piece of rail from one place to another, we were also given gigantic tongs to grasp it—two laborers to each pair, four pair of tongs along each twenty foot section of track. Hence it took eight American men to move the rail and to position it properly on the ties. From time to time we would see a group of Russian women prisoners also working on section gangs. On at least one occasion we saw them move a section of rail with only two pair of tongs, two women to each tong. Four Russian women were doing what it took eight American men to do. These were husky ladies.

German railroad tracks are standard gauge, as are American tracks, but they are constructed differently from those in the United States. Train tracks in the United States are supported by wooden railroad ties lying on top of a bed of cinders; these German tracks were supported by steel ties resting on a layer of aggregate, small crushed stone. The steel tie was about the same length and width as an American wooden tie, but it was flat with all four edges turned down to form a lip, rather like the lid of a shoebox. The rail was attached to the tie by a clamp- and bolt-like affair. We used a long-handled lug wrench to screw the bolt into the clamp, thus attaching the rail to the tie. The hocker and the pitchfork were principally used to maneuver the aggregate underneath the tie to align it or level it properly. We would also move the aggregate about to make sure the curves were banked correctly. We used the club end of the hocker to drive the stones under the railroad tie. The procedure was that one of the workmen would place a jack under the rail at any point where the German work master thought the track needed to be adjusted. The work master would move some distance down the track, kneel down and sight the rail as though he were aiming a gun. He determined whether it needed to be raised, lowered or left alone, and signaled his decision to the man on the jack, who would act accordingly. The POWs then used their pitchforks and hockers to either drive aggregate up under the tie or remove it, whichever was required to support the rail at the correct level and pitch. Some of the guys became experts at driving a hocker against the rail in such a way as to break the handle. If the German work master or one of the guards was looking, the POW would throw his hands up in frustration and despair—this having been an obvious accident. On the other hand, if only his buddies were looking, he would crack the biggest grin in town. This was just another of our small contributions to the German war effort.

Another, less successful, attempt to do our part for the war effort took place one day when we were ordered to move a very large section of track from one location to another. This took nearly the entire day, but we managed to accomplish the job. The part that the Germans had not planned, however, was that prior to setting the track in its new position, our guys buried at least a dozen hockers and pitchforks in the gravel underneath it. This time though, our creative sabotage didn't last very long because a couple of weeks later we had to move the same section of track back to its original location, and this time the Germans were watching. As we dug up the section of track, we unearthed the hockers and pitchforks. The Germans had foiled our efforts without even knowing it.

The work master was a German civilian who worked for the railroad. He and I developed a rather friendly relationship, so friendly in fact that on one occasion he presented me with a curved, German-style smoking pipe. I kept that pipe throughout my stay at Stalag IV-F and brought it home with me. The work master smoked his own pipe, and it was comical indeed to see him kneeling down, sighting the rail with his curved pipe billowing smoke that hung over the edge of the rail, away from his face. I believe his generosity, though, was not totally without purpose: He thought I might be receiving American pipe tobacco in the Red Cross packages and would offer to share it with him. He was wrong; we received no pipe tobacco, so I just smoked his. The tobacco the Germans smoked was called "Russian tobacco" by both the Germans and the Americans, although I think some of the German civilians must have grown their own. Russian tobacco was nothing more than chopped up tobacco stems and it was awful, but it did suffice. The stuff was murder to roll into a cigarette because the pieces would poke through the paper.

There were other relationships between the POWs and the German personnel, particularly the German guards. Some were friendly; some were not. There was one guard who was persistently unfriendly and hostile. He was tall and skinny; his face was very pale and boney and looked like a skull sitting on top of his shoulders. We dubbed him Skull-Face. There also was a small, white-haired guard who was constantly screaming at one or another of us. Even though none of us could understand what he was saying, he was still a nuisance. We called him Pop. There was another guard, however, who appeared to be a family man and seemed to want to make friends with us. He would walk through the barracks at night just before lights out and try to talk to us in halting English and we would reply in our pidgin German. There were others there as well who were friendly— and others who were hostile.

Shortly after reveille one morning, as we were lining up in formation preparing to go to our work detail, the guard noticed that one American POW was missing. He called and called and called again, but still the American did not report to formation. The German guard reported this to the camp commander, who cavalierly took the guard's bayonet in hand and strode into the barracks. He found the POW lying on his back in his bunk. The corporal ordered him up saying, "It's time for work," but the POW informed him, "I ain't going today!" The commander did not say another word, but carefully placed the point of the bayonet in the middle of the man's stomach, being careful not to poke him, and with his other hand made an upwards motion with his thumb. The American couldn't mistake the message; he got up in a hurry and joined the formation.

. . . . .

The railroad yard at Adorf was near a military target of some importance to the Allies. Frequently in the evening British Mosquito[7] bombers and other night raiders would fly over the camp. When the bombers came, the German guards would herd us out of our barracks, away from the yard and onto a nearby hilltop where we were thought to be safe. You could almost set your watch by the British; they invariably showed up about 9:00 p.m. Often the guards would point in the direction of the explosive flashes in the distance and tell us what town had been hit. They might shake their heads and say Chemnets or

---

3 Dubbed the Wooden Wonder or Timber Terror, the Mosquito was one of the most famous aircraft of World War II. (http://www.squidoo.com/deHavillandMosquito)

77

Munsen, for example. The night bombers never struck directly at Adorf.

There were also air raids in the area during the day while we were working on the tracks. Just as with the night raids, the German guards would herd us away from the tracks to a place of safety. Strangely enough, there was never an incident when bombs fell at the location where we were working. Nevertheless, the German guards did not know where the bombs would be dropped, so they felt it necessary to move everyone to safety. I remember watching those flights of B-17s and B-24s go over. We would all look up and shout something like "Go get 'em guys!" or "Give 'em hell, Yanks!" After the bombers had passed over, a small German plane would almost invariably come by, traversing the area in a leisurely fashion, probably to assure everyone that the airstrike was over and everyone could relax. During one of these raids, a German soldier who had been passing by had plopped down on the ground next to one of the other guys and me. He looked at us and, in relatively good English, said, "The war may be about over for us (Germany), but in two months after it is, you will be in a war with Russia." He wasn't very far wrong.

Once when my crew was working in the switching yard in Adorf, a German automobile, equipped with rail-like wheels, and therefore capable of riding along the railroad tracks, arrived on the scene. An impressive looking German officer alighted from this odd vehicle and proceeded to walk across the yard toward the German work master. As he walked by, we tried to tell him that we were weak and hungry and that we needed nourishment. He looked at us disdainfully and said, "*Krieg ist krieg.*" He just kept walking and didn't look back.

Another day while we were working on the tracks in the rail yard at Adorf, a long train of cattle cars came into the yard and paused for a moment or two. The cars were loaded with civilians—men, women and children. Some of the people in the nearest car began calling out to us through the slats. Some of us answered them and one American called out, "Who are you?" One of the occupants called back, "We are Dutch." The American asked, "Deutsch?" A reply came from a different voice in the car, "*Nein, Ish bin Hollander,*" and the first voice said again "We are not German!" At the time, none of us knew exactly who these people were or where they were going, but there is little question now that they were among the millions transported to the German concentration camps.

As I mentioned earlier, each POW had a small box in which he kept all his personal belongings. And when I say, "all," I mean precisely that. Everything you had was stored in that box. These items were very precious to us, since they constituted all of our worldly possessions. Nevertheless, we had to leave them in the barracks during the day when we went out to work. Once in a while, when we returned to the barracks, one of the POWs would notice that an item was missing from his box. In spite of our efforts we were never able to determine whether there was a thief among us or whether the German guards were playing games with us. My best guess is the latter. The guards probably wanted to keep us a little uncertain about each other and to cause our morale to falter. Also it would have been quite difficult for any American to steal from another since we were all usually outside of the barracks at the same time.

Extra-Curricular Activities

The accommodations at Stalag IV-F were sparse, to say the least. Our beds were double bunks made of wood, much as children might use today. Of course they had no springs at all; they were simply wooden platforms with sides. The mattresses were burlap bags filled with straw. The hygiene was not of the highest order, either, which led inevitably to the company of creepy-crawlers in your bed. It was not unusual for a POW to awaken during the night and feel a bedbug crawling somewhere on his body. It also was not unusual for him to grasp that critter between his thumb and index finger and squash it against the upright stanchion of the bed, leaving a bloody mark. Many beds had quite a few of these records of bedbug extermination. It was a mark of heroism for a prisoner to be the one with the greatest number of marks on the side of his bunk.

One might expect that all would be harsh and dirty in a prisoner-of-war camp, but that was not the case at Stalag IV-F. There was hard work during the day of course, although we did find ways to goldbrick—and I was an expert. There were also restrictions on movement at night, but the POWs did have some forms of entertainment. There were paperback books in English that came from "somewhere." There were also poker games. I never learned to play poker, simply because I never really wanted to, but I would sometimes watch the game as a form of entertainment. One evening as I was watching, my buddies importuned me to join the fray. I protested, because I didn't know how to play, but one of my friends (a short, burly, tough boy from Detroit) said that if I had some money he would show me how to play the game. Well, I did and he did and we won a lot of money.

I should point out that that the prisoners were not entirely slave laborers; we received a fairly substantial 32 marks a month from the German government for our work. We had no idea what it was worth in American dollars, but we knew it couldn't be much. The money was practically useless to us anyway, since the only things we could buy were German beer—*sans* alcohol—onions and mustard. The beer was awful, but it did provide something to drink and we looked forward to the keg that arrived on Sunday. When the wagon went in for food on Sunday mornings, we would pool our money and send it in with the detail. They would buy the beer and bring it back to us. The onions and the mustard gave us the ingredients for sandwiches—if and when we could find any bread to make them. We occasionally did have the bread we had been issued or had gotten from the Czech linemen. We were always a little hungry, so a sandwich of bread, onion and mustard wasn't too bad.

The bedbug problem frequently got so much out of hand that the German camp commander would order the mattresses taken out and burned and new mattresses supplied in their stead. This happened on one occasion shortly after I had placed my large roll of Deutsche marks in my mattress. One fateful afternoon when we returned from work, I noticed that my old mattress, Deutsche marks and all, was gone and in its place was a bright, new burlap bag filled with fresh straw. The loss was not a dramatic one, since, as I said, there was very little to spend one's money on.

Beer, of course, was a staple in the German diet, but unlike Americans, the Germans drink their beer at room temperature. When we would take ours outside to cool it off a little bit, the Germans would tell us, "Oh no, oh no, that will give you stomach cramps!" Of course it didn't, so we figured what we were hearing just an old wives' tale.

One interesting thing about Stalag IV-F was that it was populated entirely by American enlisted men. There were no noncommissioned officers among us, either. The rule was that officers were not permitted to work and since this was a work camp, the officers must have been quartered elsewhere. They weren't allowed to work, so I guess they just sat around and waited for the war to end. They probably had it much worse than we did. I am sure their food supply worsened even faster than ours did—the Germans wanted our labor, so it was to their advantage to feed us somewhat better than those who didn't work. The one exception to our All-American team was one guy from South Africa who arrived at the camp around mid-December. He was only with us for about a month before the Germans shipped him off to somewhere else. I don't remember his name, but we were all intrigued by this man from a country we knew nothing about. He told some funny stories about life down there.

Three of the 80 of us were paratroopers—one from the 101st Airborne Division and two from the 82nd Airborne Division. These guys held themselves aloof from the other prisoners, evidently thinking that they were somehow superior to the rest of us. One of them was a particularly aggressive young man who, during the early evenings, would frequently manage to find his way under the perimeter fence and over toward the area where the Russian women were quartered. We never knew whether he actually entered the Russian compound or whether the Russian girls came out to meet him, but it was obvious to all of us that our dauntless paratrooper was finding female companionship on a regular basis.

Those of us who shared the fellow's sleeping room realized that if he didn't show up for bed check on time, we might all have a problem with the German guards—and, given his chosen form of recreation, we couldn't trust that he'd be keeping track of the time. So without any formal decision, it became an unspoken understanding that when it was time for him to come back under the wire to meet muster at lights out, someone from the barracks would walk into the courtyard and softly whistle a tune—it didn't matter what tune. Our ideas about what he did while he was outside the fence were confirmed by the private snickering among the three paratroopers the next day. We never knew for sure, but it was a boost to our morale to believe that what we thought happened really did happen.

The paratroopers were also noted for their rabbit stew. Well, at least they were noted for their culinary expertise with rabbit meat. This resulted from an incident that occurred while we were working under a railroad bridge near the city of Bad-Elster. There were several domesticated rabbits in and around a farmyard located under the bridge. Near the end of the workday one of the paratroopers captured a big buck rabbit, hid it under his coat, and took it back to camp. There they dressed him, disposing of the hide and entrails in the latrine, and prepared a delicious rabbit dish of some sort on the pot-bellied stove. There was great anticipation among the POWs who were sitting around enjoying the aroma of the cooking. Just thinking of rabbit stew or even of a small morsel of rabbit made all of our mouths water. But the mighty paratroopers were not the least bit interested in sharing their feast with the rest of us. And so it was that everyone else in the barracks got the aroma and the paratroopers got the meat.

CHAPTER NINE
Winter 1944
Adorf, Plauen, Bad Elster

During the last months of 1944, my section gang worked principally in the area near Bad-Elster, a town fairly close to the border between Germany and what was then Czechoslovakia. On one occasion, however, we were dispatched to the rail yards near the rail center at Plauen. The yards there had sustained significant damage in several Allied air raids and we were to augment the regular crews that worked the surrounding area. When we arrived at Plauen, we saw destruction beyond belief. If you had never seen a city that has been bombed, you would not have believed your eyes. The damage was beyond imagination—far worse than a tornado or a hurricane would have produced. Our job was to clean up the rubbish that was the aftermath of the bombing raids—brick, stone, rails, jagged pieces of concrete and other debris to clear the tracks. We worked in the Plauen area at least two days, perhaps more, and the memory will stay with me forever: the stench of cordite, burned wood and death—an odor so distinct that once you have experienced it, you never forget it.

One day our work gang was summoned to a location near an offloading station that had sustained a visit from a single bomber, evidently with a single bomb. The work train backed up almost to the spot in the middle of the track where there was a tremendous crater. Our flyer friend had made his mark; as we offloaded the train we saw the happy sight. We had our tools with us, but the Germans had us to stand off to the side while they conferred with each other. There was quite a collection of military brass at the site, and standing among them was our little old white-haired guard we called Pop. For some stupid reason, I decided to jump down into the crater and start digging with the pick end of my hocker. When Pop saw me, he also jumped into the crater, ran over to where I was and started to shout in my ear at the top of his lungs to stop what I was doing and get back with the others. I did, but a few minutes later I tried the same thing again, with the same result. I think old Pop was about to blow his top right in front of all the brass. At the rather strong suggestion of one of our guys, I didn't do it anymore. I could have gotten all of us in trouble. Or worse, there might have been other unexploded bombs buried where I was digging. I don't think the Germans wanted the hole any deeper anyway. As is typical of engineers and government officials, after we stood around waiting for most of

the morning, they loaded us back onto the same work train and took us back to finish the job at the same place we had been the day before.

One of our work locations close to the city of Bad-Elster was by the side of a country inn. When it was time for our lunch break, we sat on the back veranda of the Inn. While we were eating, and for a little while afterwards, we were given almost free rein to move in and about the building. I wandered into the kitchen where, in sign language or in broken English and German, a German woman who was preparing food asked if I would like a bowl of soup. I indicated that I would and she provided a bowl of thick, hot, delicious soup. That—and some bread she gave me to go with it—was undoubtedly the best meal I had had in months. In an effort to express my thanks, I took from my pocket the wad of Deutsche Marks I had saved from my ill-fated poker game and offered her the entire roll. The money didn't mean anything to me and I thought it would be helpful to her. She indicated she wanted only a few of the German marks, not the entire roll. I thought I was making a friendly gesture and insisted she take the entire roll, since the money was of no real use to me. The lady, rather than accepting the money, became indignant. She opened the door to the fire chamber of the coal-fired stove, and pantomimed, "Do you think our money is only worth putting in the stove to burn?" I apologized again and got out of there as quickly as I could while I was ahead.

When I left the kitchen, instead of going back to the veranda, I went exploring in the inn. As I was wandering the halls hoping to see something of interest (maybe a female) a voice behind me said, "Hello, who are you?" This was said in German, but by now I understood that much. I turned around to see who was attached to the voice and found a German officer, in full dress uniform, walking with a cane and missing part of his right arm. As I was turning I tried to think up an excuse for being there, but before I had time to answer, the officer was pointing to my watch. He was very friendly, and in some German that I could understand, he offered to buy it. This was the watch my parents had given me when I left for the Army Induction Center at Ft. MacPherson—the same watch I had successfully concealed when I was originally captured. I could see he really wanted the watch. He said he wanted it for his wife. In spite of a generous offer of one hundred cigars, which would have bought more bread or other stuff than I could have carried back into camp in a year, I thought it best to decline the offer and keep my treasured watch. As might be expected, he would not take no for an answer and kept trying to negotiate the purchase. I continued to say, "No, no, my *mutter* and *vater* give to me. No, no, cannot sell. My *mutter* and *vater* give to me." He finally got the message and turned away. I got the hell out of there and back to the comfort of our German guards. I still have that treasured watch.

Each morning when the German guards would meet the German work master at the work site, they would all raise their right arms and give the standard German greeting, "*Heil* Hitler." We Americans would mimic the Germans by doing likewise to one another, but our greeting would be, "*Heil* Roosevelt." Most of the time the Germans didn't get the joke and thought that was our usual greeting.

These are some of the Deutsch Marks I earned working on the railroad.

One morning when we walked up to the passenger platform preparing to board the train for our daily work detail, a couple of the guys starting acting as though they were refusing board the train. On that particular day we only had one guard. He kept trying to coax the guys onto the train as it was about to leave, but we could tell that he didn't know what to do. As the train whistle gave one last toot, the frustrated guard looked the first guy in the eye and very directly worked the bolt action on his rifle, which would have placed a round in the firing chamber. With that, no more was said and everyone boarded the train very quickly. As I think about it now, I doubt if he even had any bullets in his rifle and was afraid we might not take the bluff and someone would see that he had lost control of his prisoners.

On one occasion, after taking cover from approaching bombers, we heard rumblings far to the east; an air raid was being conducted somewhere close to the Czech border. The following day, we discovered what and where the rumblings had been. The border between Germany and Czechoslovakia at Bad Elster is the Elbe River—a stream perhaps 150 to 200 yards wide. There had been an air raid on a railroad bridge crossing the river from eastern Germany into western Czechoslovakia. We were dispatched to help repair the bridge. When we arrived, we saw a major two-track, stone railroad bridge spanning the Elbe. The bridge had sustained noticeable damage about midway across. It was obvious that many bombs had been dropped because the surrounding area was pockmarked with craters. It looked like pictures we see today of the surface of the moon. Only a few of the bombs had hit the span itself, but they had caused damage significant enough to put the bridge out of operation. Our crew, along with other POWs and other laborers, had been brought in to restore the bridge to operational status.

The bridge was a massive stone structure supported by several arches underneath the rail bed. The damage appeared to be principally to the rail bed, since the supporting arches were still intact. There was probably damage to the upper portions of the arches that would require replacement of mortar and other such repair, but all in all, the structure appeared to be reasonably sound. The barriers along the sides of the bridge, however, had sustained considerable damage.

We spent several days on top of the bridge standing on the crushed rock roadbed, kicking one foot against the other to try to keep the blood circulating, shivering and trying to stay warm any way we could. We even shoveled some of the gravel into trucks for removal. One particular morning when we climbed down from the work train the German work master came over to where we were, pointed at three of my buddies and me, and indicated that he wanted us to follow him. We had been selected as special assistants to a crew of German stonemasons, whose job was to make repairs to the stone works at the tops of the archways under the bridge where mortar had been shaken loose by the exploding bombs. This was no place for anyone who was afraid of heights. Our work was conducted on scaffolding well over 100 feet high. The scaffold was built from the ground up to the archway, and believe me, it was a considerable distance up in the air. To reach the work platform we had to climb up ladders from level to level to get to the top of the scaffold. It was late 1944, in the middle of the continent of Europe. The work area was wide open to the elements. It was cold and blustery and the conditions up there were not pleasant, to say the least. The German stone workers, however, had with them on the scaffold a steel basket of sorts, containing a large amount of coke that burned brightly in the wind and provided a great deal of warmth to them, and to us as we worked nearby. Thus, we were more comfortable working on the platform than the laborers who were working on the top of the bridge.

The work we were performing under the bridge was difficult at best. We had to take pneumatic jackhammers, hoist them in the air over our heads and bore holes in the mortar area between the stones of the bridge. Once the hole was bored sufficiently, we would insert a hose and pump viscous, wet mortar into the hole, thus strengthening the bridge. I have lost track of how long we were there, but it could have been at least two or three weeks that the four of us did this type of work on that scaffold in the cold German winter wind. The workers were allowed a break at midmorning, one at lunch, and one in the middle of the afternoon. This meant that they—and we—ascended several hundred feet of scaffolding at least three times a day and descended a similar number of times, with short periods in between filled with difficult work that simply could not be avoided.

The Germans called the morning break *frühstück*, the German word for breakfast. After the laborious descent down the ladders, the entire crew—Germans and Americans—went into a small shack at the base of the bridge. There was little heat in the shack, but it was out of the elements. The German stonemasons treated us as friends, but there wasn't much conversation between them and us because we didn't speak their language, nor did they speak ours. The stonemasons each had a little lunchbox with some of the typical German bread and orange marmalade or something else to spread on it. Often they would have an apple. And, as always, they each had a container of ersatz coffee. They ate very sparingly—I guess because they had very little and it had to go a long way. We didn't have any food, but at least we were not up on that scaffold and the atmosphere was friendly. About the second morning, we entered the shack and found our seats at the other end of the old table from the Germans. As they started to take their goodies from their lunchboxes, one of them looked up and saw us watching them. We must have looked like puppies staring up from under the dinner table. One of them turned to the fellow sitting beside him and said something in German. (We could not quite understand what he said, but we had a pretty good idea.) Then he turned to us with his hand out offering a small piece of his bread. I didn't hesitate to accept it and with that, the other Germans did likewise with my buddies. One of the German workers even gave me an apple! After that, we began to bring little things from the Red Cross packages to share with our new friends. This, then, became a routine exchange.

While working on the bridge, we noticed a German training camp of some sort across the river in Czechoslovakia. We knew it was a training camp because we would frequently observe German soldiers, probably officers, marching in formation, counting cadence and singing. The purpose of the camp was a mystery, but as the days went on, from time to time—especially on clear days—we could see some type of aircraft flying very high overhead. There was something very strange about these planes, though, because they seemed to be flying far, far in advance of the point from which their engine noise emanated. The aircraft would appear to be far to our left, while the engine noise was coming from our right. It was not until much later, after I was back home, that I realized that these had been experimental jet aircraft that the Germans were beginning to manufacture, and that the aircraft itself was so fast that it far outdistanced the sound it was making, light, of course, travelling far faster than sound. Although this was only a supposition, looking back on it, it seems to have been an accurate one.

Christmas, 1944, was a great event for the American POWs. We had been advised by our captors that we would have a couple of days off to observe the Christmas holiday. Shortly before the holidays began, I made a particular effort to collect cigarettes from my friends who wanted me to bring in their loaf of special holiday bread. Actually, the bread would be no different from what I usually brought in, but this would be for their feast. The Czechoslovakian linemen who rode the work train with us were also preparing for their holiday sale of bread. On the last workday prior to the Christmas holidays, I took all of these cigarettes with me and managed to trade them for eight loaves of delicious German bread. Believe it or not, I managed to conceal this entire cache of bread beneath my greatcoat, in my trousers and elsewhere under my clothing, and bring it back to camp undetected. Of course the effort was not entirely altruistic; I kept one of the loaves for myself.

On January 1, 1945, it began to snow in Adorf, and it continued to snow for the entire month of January. During this period, we were often rousted out of the barracks at night and ordered to the nearby rail yards to chip ice off of the railroad switches. To do this we used a strange broom-like device with a sharp metal spike on one end of the broomstick and a heavy broom on the other. We used the spike end to break up the ice and the broom end to sweep it off the track. Winter in Central Europe produced many hardships and this was but one of them. Standing on steel crossties and rock roadbed in shoes whose soles were growing thinner and thinner was no joy, believe me. The engines that pulled the trains in this part of Germany during the winter of 1944 and 1945 were old, dilapidated steam engines. They generated an abundance of extraneous moisture that would envelop them in the cold air as they came into town. In fact, when a train came down the tracks, it was likely that you would not see the engine at all, just a mass of steam and fog pulling a long line of cars. By this time, the Germans had begun hooking two and sometimes three locomotives to their trains. So much steam was leaking from the engines that they could not keep the pressure high enough in any single engine to pull the load.

The Germans also used another, strange-looking, vehicle in and around Adorf—a steam-powered truck. The truck's bed held a wood-burning apparatus that produced the steam to run the truck. On at least one occasion, one of the POWs from our camp was sent off on a work detail to chop wood to burn in these trucks.

One day when we were working on the tracks alongside the main street leading into Adorf, I saw a sight that almost made my eyes pop out. I was resting and leaning on my pitchfork when I looked up to see a truckload of beef going down the street. Through the open back of the van I could see rows of quarters of fresh beef hanging on meat hooks. The German guard standing nearby looked at me and saw what I was looking at. He smiled at me and said *Einem Stück* (one piece). Believe me, he too had a wishful gleam in his eye.

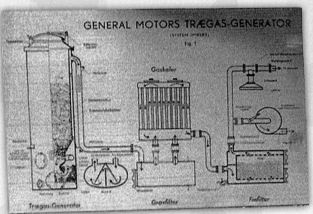

This is a steam truck similar to the one I described. I took this picture while on vacation in Denmark in 1985.

CHAPTER TEN
The Beginning of the End

In early 1945 my crew was often assigned to work in the railroad yards at Adorf, particularly in and around the roundhouse itself. For the most part, our job was simply to tidy up the area, pick up trash and debris and serve as general custodians of the yard. Oddly enough, during the time we were working in the yard, the German work master began to give us daily reports on the development of the war. It became standard practice for him, first thing in the morning when he would greet us, to give us a report on the progress of the American armies, which were coming toward Adorf from the west. He called the American armies "Eisenhower" and would tell us in German—sometimes understood and sometimes not—Eisenhower 's position, or how many kilometers Eisenhower had advanced since the day before, or how many kilometers west of Adorf Eisenhower was. He did not appear to be angry at all about what he was telling us. On the contrary, he reported the Allies' advance rather cheerfully. It seemed as if he realized that the war was about end and was doing everything he could to put himself in our good graces.

And so it was that the winter of 1945 moved inexorably on. Our activities in February and March were much the same as they had been in December and January—except that the soup was getting thinner and thinner. It was not until mid-April that things started to get exciting.

The first thing that happened was that one evening, probably around the eighteenth or the twentieth of April, one of the guards wandered into our day room with a very downtrodden expression on his face and told us that President Roosevelt had died. At first we didn't believe him, but it was easy to see he was deadly serious and very sad. All he could do was repeat, "Good man, good man." Then he told us that the new president was some guy named Truman. None of us had ever heard of Mr. Truman and we were shaking our heads and asking each other, "Who the hell is he?" Actually, Roosevelt had died on April 12, just 83 days after he had begun his unprecedented fourth term in office.

A few days later, on a bright, beautiful early spring Sunday morning, we were enjoying our regular day of leisure. It was so sunny that many of our guys had arisen early and begun washing clothes and generally relaxing as we were wont to do on Sunday. (There were, of course, no religious services for any of us.) Some of the guys were talking about going outside and stretching out on the little bit of grass that was starting to grow in front of the barracks. It was still a little too cold for me to want to sunbathe, but these guys were Yankees and didn't know any better.

Suddenly we heard the sound of aircraft approaching from the northwest. We knew immediately that these were not German put-puts; these were real airplanes. As the sounds of the engines grew louder and louder, we could hear machine gun fire, interspersed with the boom of the accompanying 20 mm cannons being fired from the aircraft. Although we had been away from combat for many months, we all recognized the sound of aircraft strafing an area. The plane would approach the target, fire a burst from their weapons, pull up and away, then turn around and come back for another run. The sound was unmistakable. As the planes came in low over the camp with guns blazing, we could hear them bank, make their turn and come back for another hit. As if on cue, all of us hit the deck, scrambling for cover. If we had been able to, we would have crawled into the cracks in the floor—of which there were many. I found myself under a table in the day room looking at my friend Olson who, in a single motion, had dropped into position as though he had been expecting the necessity at any moment.

We could not see what was going on because the camp was separated from the railroad yards by the gravity-flow switching hill, so we were unsure what the target of the strafing operation was, but the sound of the gunfire was ominous. Later it became obvious that the target had been the railroad yards, particularly the roundhouse and the several engines parked there. At the beginning of the raid there had been at least seven or eight—perhaps as many as 12—steam engines parked near the roundhouse awaiting repairs and service. It was impossible to see the extent of damage, but it was clear that none of those engines would move again until after until the end of the war. In all probability, no German trains in that sector would move again because by that time anything that moved was a sure target for American aircraft.

When the German camp commander heard the strafing operation start, he ran out of his office, flung open the gate to the compound, as if to provide a way of escape for the American prisoners, then ran back into his office and hid under the stove until the strafing operation stopped. Leaning out the window with some sort of automatic weapon, a German soldier stationed in the tower of the roundhouse tried to mount some defense against the American raid. He didn't bring down any aircraft, but apparently he got their attention because the entire wall surrounding his window was covered with 20 mm cannon and 50-caliber bullet holes.

It was over in just a few minutes and the aircraft went away. After the noise had faded, as we pulled ourselves out from whatever we had found to hide under, simultaneous laughter broke out from every quarter of our rooms. We couldn't stop. It was wild. This went on for a good twenty minutes until someone asked, "What's happening? What should we do?" As we began to simmer down, we realized that what had happened to the roundhouse might have happened to the other part of Stalag IV-F. All of a sudden everyone raced outdoors. All the POWs poured out of the barracks and all the guards and the camp CO rushed out of their office building. In all the excitement we didn't feel like guards and prisoners. We were all occupants of the same place; we were all in this thing together. We looked around and found there had been no damage to the buildings and no one had been injured, a fact for which we all breathed a sigh of relief. We did find evidence that one ricochet shell had hit in the middle of the parade ground, but that was all. The guys flying those P-52s must have known we were down there.

After the air raid, we held a series of meetings—without the German camp personal— aimed at planning for some protection in the event that ground troops approached the camp. We did not want to be caught in a crossfire between advancing Allies and defending Germans. Several ideas were tossed out. One was to dig slit trenches or foxholes in the parade ground and along the fence. Another was to dig out the latrine, since there were heavy timbers already around an excavation. But this was a stinking idea and we gave it up. We also decided it would be good idea to establish a watch, so we would know when we needed to take protective measures.

Not long after we began to hold these meetings, the German authorities herded all the camp inmates together and moved us out of Stalag IV-F into a nearby wooded area, where we stayed for several days. Not only were we Americans there, but other people—unknown, but obviously prisoners—were also being herded into the area. It is difficult to say why this evacuation took place, but it seemed likely that it was for the protection of the prisoners in case there was another raid on the rail yard. It was quite possible that the Germans feared the American planes would return and bomb the area again.

We had spent a number of days in the forest when a contingent of *Hitler-Jugend* (Hitler Youth) appeared on the scene. These were young boys, teenagers or younger, dressed in black uniforms with swastika armbands on their left arms and carrying machine pistols. They were a fearsome lot, even though they were young, because it was obvious that they had been thoroughly indoctrinated and that they were not the least bit reluctant to use their weapons. As I think back on the situation, I expect the little bastards were looking for a chance to do just that. Hence, we got the message and heeded the instructions of these young thugs as they herded us back to Stalag IV-F.

By April, 1945, the Germans were obviously beginning to feel tremendous pressure from the Allied forces advancing from the west and the Russian forces advancing through Poland and Czechoslovakia from the east. It was as if they were being compressed in a massive vise. As the Russians advanced and neared the prisoner-of-war camps, the Germans would remove the prisoners from the camps, form them into marching units and march them toward the west. On the other side of the front, as the Allied forces advanced, the Germans would remove those prisoners and put them on the road marching east. There was a continuous flow of prisoners on the roads, converging in the general area of the Germans POW camps. It remained this way, the compression becoming more and more acute, until liberation place in April and May. But I was not to liberation.

I did not receive this letter until after I returned home.

94

CHAPTER ELEVEN
The Clinic

Apparently the Germans were planning to put everyone from Stalag IV-F on the road for the duration of the war because after we were returned to the camp by the Hitler Youth, the camp commander began making arrangements to do exactly that. While we were out in the woods, however, I had developed a sore on the top of my left foot. I asked permission from the CO to go to the nearby clinic, a small operation run by a French doctor and a French Catholic priest that had been established by the Germans to serve as a central medical facility for prisoners-of-war throughout the area. It was a barracks-like structure with a treatment room of sorts at one end, a day room of sorts at the other, and a row of double-deck bunks in between. When I arrived, the doctor treated the sore on my foot, applying some medication and covering the sore with a bandage. It really was not a very big sore; I was able to put on my shoe and walk without any significant discomfort. Nevertheless, when the doctor asked me if I'd like to remain at the clinic, without blinking an eye I said, "Sure would," and was assigned a bunk near the treatment room. There were perhaps 15 to 20 other POW patients with me—several Americans, as well as Australians, New Zealanders, Englishmen and Canadians. Nobody seemed to be very sick.

That night after dark, two German soldiers came in and began to speak to the doctor and the priest. I felt sure they were looking for me, so I lay quiet in my bunk and did not stir. The Frenchmen told the Germans I was not there. The next day, they told me what had happened, but I, like Brer Rabbit in the Uncle Remus stories, "just lay low." To my delight, I had found a home—at least for a while.

On the second day of my residence at the clinic, another American and I decided to take a walk. We walked down the hillside and into the little town of Adorf. Nobody seemed to pay us any mind as we wandered through the streets, so we continued on, just as though we belonged there. While walking along looking for we did not know what, we decided to try our luck at one of the houses. One house that sat away from its neighbors looked appealing. It was a little one-story grey building with probably two bedrooms and the other typical rooms found in such a house. We walked around back, knocked on the back door and were greeted by an elderly German housewife. She invited us to come in and share some food with her. She did not speak any English, but the sign language was effective;

we accepted politely and went in. Just as she started to make us something to eat, she saw something through the window and suddenly turned pale as a ghost. My companion saw it, too. He turned to me and whispered in my ear, "There are Hitler Youth out there." We quietly slipped out the back door and made our way up the hill to the Clinic, hoping the lady would not suffer any mistreatment from those nasty little *Hitler-Jugend* as payment for her kindness to us.

As we were reentering the clinic, we encountered two German soldiers who were just leaving. One of them looked at my unshaven face and asked, *"Nein Messer?"* (No razor?) I just looked at him, shrugged my shoulders and kept walking.

CHAPTER TWELVE
Escape, Recapture, and Escape Again

The next day, the French doctor called all of us patients together in the dayroom and told us that he was going to take four of us to within one kilometer of the American lines. Then he took out a deck of playing cards, spread them out face down on the table and told us each to pick one card. The four highest draws would determine which of us would accompany him. Guess who was one of the four high-card pickers? Me.

The next morning around breakfast time, the doctor took four patients—a Britisher, a New Zealander, an Australian and me—and started out by foot, headed west toward the American lines. The fact that we were of four different nationalities was pure coincidence; we were just the lucky ones—chosen solely on the basis of who had drawn the four highest cards. The doctor was very careful to skirt any area where we would stand out. He had made sure that we did not have knapsacks or other parcels that would look suspicious. We took only what we could carry in our pockets.

The walk took at least an hour, perhaps two. Eventually we came upon a heavily wooded area through which we walked for a while until we were deep into the woods. There we encountered a group of perhaps 15 to 20 French POWs who had escaped from their camp. They were noticeably loud and boisterous, and laden with personal possessions that they had brought with them. They had suitcases, pots and pans, bags and every other thing imaginable. We wondered how they could have escaped from anywhere, except maybe a circus. The doctor told us to join these French escapees because we were now only one kilometer from the American lines and they would take us through. We did as we were told. We had come this far with the doctor and we figured, "What the hell?" So we joined the Frenchmen and the entire group proceeded to walk through the wooded area. The Frenchmen were noisy; they sounded like a herd of wild elephants. Nevertheless, we followed along as we had been told to do.

After walking for about fifteen or twenty minutes we reached a clearing. As we approached it, all seemed quiet—except our French companions. We could see a wide, clear field covered with some low-growing plants, maybe grass or grain. Across the field was another wooded area. Our thought was to make it across the open field and into the woods on the other side. The French POWs headed out into the clearing as though they were going to a Sunday picnic. As the last of the group reached the edge of the clearing, we heard a resounding "HALT! HALT!" We all stopped dead in our tracks; those words carried a meaning we all understood. We looked around and discovered, almost immediately, that we had walked through a series of camouflaged German foxholes. We had escaped right into a German outpost occupied by German infantrymen. The Germans poured from their foxholes and rounded us up like cattle. After looking us over and deciding that we were harmless and had nothing they wanted, they escorted us toward the area to their rear. Two or three infantrymen guarded us as we were returned to the east. Soon we reached a small schoolhouse and were ordered into it. We were marched into the school's auditorium and told to remain there until someone came to get us and escort us back to our prison camps.

The auditorium reminded me of the one in my old Eatonton High School. It had the typical stage with seating out front for about fifty students. We, along with the French, were seated in the audience area. Another group of recaptured escapees was seated on the stage. These were Polish or Czechoslovakian forced laborers who had tried to escape. As soon as the German guards departed, the people on the stage quietly eased out of the schoolhouse, leaving all of their belongings behind. The last of this bunch had hardly gone through the door when the French escapees bounded onto the stage and rummaged through the personal effects searching for new treasures to add to their burgeoning collections. While the French were joyously picking through the paraphernalia, the New Zealander, the Australian, the Brit and I slipped quietly out of the schoolhouse and made our way laboriously back to the clinic.

As we were walking, we came upon a small house on the right side of the road. We approached the house and saw an old woman standing beside it. She saw us as well and motioned for us to come toward her. When we reached her, she asked in a guttural accent, "Would you like some milk?" Would we? Of course we would—who wouldn't? We were always ready to eat—or drink—and happily indicated that we would love some milk. The woman took us around to the side of the house, reached down and lifted a fitted wooden cover off the ground. This turned out to be the lid of a large earthenware jar that was buried below the surface. She took a ladle in her hand, dipped into the jar and brought out cool, fresh milk, which she offered us, and which we drank with great pleasure. We all told her *danke schoen* and continued on our way toward the clinic.

A short distance later, we came across a small group of German soldiers eating a meal at a German field kitchen by the side of the road. The sun was high and we realized it must have been about noon. The Germans had formed a sort of cafeteria line and food was being dished out to them as they passed in front of a row of serving pans. By this time we had become quite bold, so the four of us simply walked up, picked up metal plates and utensils, made our way through the line and received a very delicious, hot German meal. The Germans seemed not to mind and didn't bother us at all. After we were served, the four of us found a suitable spot slightly apart from the German soldiers, sat down on the ground and ate our lunch. When we finished, we deposited our utensils in the designated place, gave a slight wave of thanks and said goodbye. As we were leaving, still heading back to the clinic, one of the Germans trotted over toward us and waved for us to stop. I thought, "Uh-oh, we have trouble!" As it turned out, he wanted to give us a warning. He told us in stilted English, "You fellows should stay off the road. There are members of the SS in the area who are shooting escaped POWs on sight." We thanked him for his help and warning and then we took off. Although this information was of some concern to us, we did not heed it, but stayed on the roadway and ultimately found our way back to the clinic.

When we finally reached home, it was just almost dark. We were greeted by the French doctor who asked what in the name of heaven had happened. We explained the whole series of events, to which his response was, "*Krieg ist krieg*!" Then he said, "All right, come on back in; your old bunks are waiting for you." The four of us went in, found some leftover food and then went to our bunks, climbed in and had a good night's sleep.

The next morning at breakfast, as I sat with the Australian, George Chapman, and the New Zealander, Pat Horne, we talked about our adventure of the day before. Both of my companions had been captured in North Africa some three years earlier, so they had over two years seniority as prisoners over me, but this made no difference. As we rehashed the preceding day's events, we noted how easy the whole thing would have been if not for the Frenchmen, and began to wonder whether we should try again. As the conversation developed, we agreed that we knew the lay of the land surrounding the camp. We knew where the German outpost was and where the American lines were. And we believed we could do it again on our own—and much more successfully than we had done the day before. We talked about whether we should ask the Brit if he wanted to try it again and decided it would be the only fair thing to do, but he said once was enough for him and that he would stay at the clinic and let whatever happened happen.

So we set out, again heading west along the same route we had used with the French doctor the preceding day. When we reached the spot in the woods where we had met the Frenchmen, we could still see signs of that herd of elephants. We stopped and looked around to locate the German outpost and then moved out again. We were much more careful this time; we walked cautiously, stealthily and with a concerted effort to be as quiet and unobtrusive as possible. Our old infantry smarts were coming back to us. We soon found ourselves approaching the edge of the woods that we had traversed the preceding day. However, we were now well aware that there was a German outpost on the eastern edge of the area, so we carefully walked far to the right and around the vicinity where we knew the outpost to be. We soon reached the clearing, but at a point about two hundred yards to the right of where we had been recaptured the day before. This time, though, we had the benefit of that unplanned reconnaissance mission. Just the same, we paused at the edge of the woods before entering the clearing to make certain that we were not walking into the same trap again.

The clearing itself was a farm field that had once been tilled, but had obviously not been plowed lately. It was several hundred yards wide and we estimated it would take 10 to 15 minutes to cross it at a normal walking pace. Before taking that first step, we held a little conference and determined that there were three possible outcomes to crossing this field: We could be shot in the back; a German soldier could call to us to stop and return; we could make it safely to the other side. We were apprehensive, but decided to make an effort to reach the American lines. Once again we figured, "What the Hell?" We started walking across the field in sort of a single file. We did not run; we did not walk quickly or slowly; we just walked steadily forward toward the western edge of the field as though we expected nothing to happen—and nothing did.

When we reached the woods on the other side of the field, we decided to take a rest and have a look around. We all flopped down on the ground, but we could see a small town down a hillock to our left. To our right in the west, we saw an autobahn that looked to us like the wide open world and safety. We decided that it would not be a good idea to head toward the town because it appeared to be on a line with the outpost we had just bypassed, and we reasoned that there would be German soldiers there. (We learned later that there were indeed soldiers in the town—American soldiers.) Instead, we headed straight for the autobahn, thinking that there we would find safety and easily reach the American lines to the west.

But once again, it was not to be. Just as we reached the autobahn and began to cross it, we heard a loud, gruff German voice to our right hollering at us. We turned and saw a German soldier with an automatic machine pistol hanging from his shoulder waving for us to come to him. There was not much we could do except follow his orders. He was a youngster about our age and not particularly hostile. After settling the fact that we were his prisoners and he was taking us to his field headquarters, he actually became quite chatty. He motioned us to follow him, which we did. A short time later, we found ourselves at a German encampment where he told us to wait until he could confer with his superiors concerning what should be done with us. I found it interesting that while there were many German soldiers milling around in the area where we had been left waiting to learn our fate, they didn't even seem to notice us. In a few minutes our captor returned and said, "Come. Come."

We did not know where the soldier was taking us but we followed along. Actually, the four of us just strolled along together. He was trying out his English and we were trying to talk him into surrendering to us. What else was there to do? There were German soldiers everywhere.

As we walked down the road, the four of us—one German, one American, one Australian and one New Zealander—engaged in the sort of conversation that might be expected from youngsters our age. I said to the German, "You know the war is almost over. Why don't you just come with us? You'd be much better off with the Americans than you would be with the Germans. If you stay here, you may very well be killed as the Americans advance." He just laughed and said, "Well, that might not be a bad idea but, really, in a couple of weeks, I am going on furlough back to Berlin to see my sweetheart. I'd much rather be with her than with you."

About nightfall, we arrived at a small village and the German took the three POWs into the center of the town to what appeared to be a civilian jail, and turned us over to the German constable in charge. The German constable greeted us and took custody of us; the soldier waved goodbye and headed back to his unit. The constable took us into the jail, told us to go into a cell where there were three bunks, and to lie down and go to sleep. We went into the cell and lay down. We followed his orders without any idea of what would happen to us the next day. The constable pushed the barred door shut but did not lock it, turned and went away. The next morning we were awakened, by the same constable, to a beautiful spring day. We had a cup of coffee with him, then he said goodbye and we walked casually out of the jail as if we owned the place.

Again we headed west. No one stood in our way. No one spoke to us or tried to stop us. In these waning days of April 1945, it was obvious to everyone that the war would soon be over and that the Allies would be the victors. There was no actual combat going on anymore in the European Theater. There were fanatics in the countryside, but most of the Germans that I encountered were not of that nature. They were not hostile and not bent on killing Americans just to be killing Americans. In fact, they wanted to do whatever they could to convince us that they were not really Nazis, but were actually pro-American. If you believe that, I'll be happy to make you the King of Austria.

We three escapees plodded on westward, determining our direction by the sun. I figured the sun rose in the east and set in the west in Germany just like it did in Eatonton (a bit of my Boy Scout training coming into play). We really had no idea precisely where we were going. We just headed west, thinking that surely we would encounter some American troops sooner or later. We carefully avoided the roadways and stuck to the fields, which were easy to negotiate, having once been farms. I remember walking through one field, down into a small valley, crossing a small stream and then ascending a small hillock on the other side. It reminded me of some of my days as a farmer back home.

It was an uneventful all-day trek. We encountered no one, friend or foe. We didn't have anything to eat but we were so intent on finding the Americans that I guess we just didn't worry about food. Toward nightfall we found a heavily wooded area and decided it would be a safe and comfortable place to spend the night. Being late April, it was still a bit chilly and the three of us had only the clothes on our backs. We had no blankets, overcoats or anything else that could serve as sleeping gear, but I remembered (again from my Boy Scout days) that the best way to stay warm while sleeping under these conditions is to take your shoes off and curl up on your side in a fetal position, so that is what we did. We slept fitfully through the night and awakened at sunrise.

The wooded area was much like all the woods we had seen during our stay in Germany: clear of underbrush and debris, with only the trees in the area providing cover. Looking back on that night, I wonder why German woods were so clear of underbrush. It could have been simply a means of keeping the woods clean, or it could have been that the woods had been scoured inch by inch over the past few years by civilians looking for firewood.

As it turned out, the "wooded" area in which we had been sleeping was quite open. In the daylight we could see that we had camped right next to a paved roadway, totally exposed and easily seen by any passersby. Fortunately there appeared to have been no passersby. We were feeling the lack of food and this would have been a great time for a hot cup of coffee and half a dozen sunny-side-up eggs, but that was only a pipe dream. We decided to proceed further west along the road. We walked for quite some time, hoping to come across something to eat. There was absolutely no traffic, pedestrian or otherwise, on the road, but soon we began to see German houses alongside it. As we passed more and more houses, we noticed that each of them had a white flag flying from an upper window, obviously indicating that the occupants wanted to surrender to the American forces. As I think about it now, the German civilians must have been scared to death of what might happen to them at the hands of the Allies.

We continued walking along the road, still headed west. Suddenly two American GIs carrying standard American M1 rifles jumped up from the ditches where they had been posted on either side of the road as guards. They halted us with their weapons drawn and asked in a commanding voice, "Who in the hell are you?" to which I answered, "I thought I was an American." But I was clearly dressed differently from the two of them. They were wearing Eisenhower jackets, a relatively new innovation in American Army uniforms. I, of course, was wearing the old standard 1942 field jacket that had been issued to me by the Germans, still fully equipped with the orange triangle in the center of the back. There was one additional feature on my jacket: a bullet hole about breast high, which probably accounted for how the Germans happened to have had the jacket in the first place. These two GIs had probably never seen an old field jacket like the one I was wearing.

The two American GIs and I conversed comfortably in English, but it was necessary for me to show them my GI dog tags in order to prove that I was in fact who I said I was. Once they were satisfied with my identity, they accepted my word as to who my companions were and radioed back to their base for instructions. They were directed that one of them should guide us to their base and then return to the outpost.

After I returned home, I was told that my mother had been overheard to say, "Frederick would never do a thing like try to escape." She was wrong.

CHAPTER THIRTEEN
Repatriation

A tall sandy-haired kid took us to a rear check point—a building that must have been an abandoned house—where an American officer took us into custody. After assuring himself that we were, in fact, escaped Allied POWs, he looked me in the eye and said, "Would you boys like to have a drink?" I responded quickly with "Yes Sir!" Then he asked whether we preferred Black and White or White Horse Scotch Whisky. We told him it really didn't make any difference; none of us had had an alcoholic beverage for quite some time. The fact was, I had never tasted whiskey in my life. I did sample the officer's brew. It tasted good and proved to be the first of many such tastes to come.

With drinks in hand we sat down and the officer debriefed us. We could tell him very little that was not already known to G2 (Army Intelligence). We did tell him about the other POWs at the clinic. When we had answered several questions about the area around the clinic, the number of German soldiers in that vicinity, and our recollection of hearing what sounded like a long gun firing somewhere nearby, he decided not to take action. The war would be over in a very few days and he felt that any engagement at this point wouldn't be worth the risk or the effort. After he ensured that the three of us received food, cigarettes and new clothes, my escape companions, the New Zealander and the Australian, were given transportation to units of the British Army and I was given a billet in a nearby building, evidently some sort of dormitory. There I found myself in the company of two British soldiers, one an Egyptian and the other an Englishman. The Egyptian fellow had one notable item among his possessions: a five-gallon GI water can half full of red wine. The three of us drank a considerable portion of two and a half gallons of red wine. We also had enough food, K-rations and other items, to make it a real party.

In the days that followed I would meet other ex-POWs, some of whom had been liberated by the Russians. It was generally known that liberation by the Russians rather than by the Americans included unexpected fringe benefits. The German civilians knew full well how German troops had treated Russian civilians during their advance into the Soviet Union in 1941 and were deathly afraid of the Russian soldiers. Assuming that the American POWs would stake out a territory and that the Russians would honor it, the civilians, especially the young women, sought the protection of the American soldiers. As a result, an American ex-POW newly liberated by the Russians often had the pleasure of making merry for a few days—or a week or two—in the home of a German *fraulein*. Not to be outdone, the rest of us soon learned that all one needed to do was to tell the townspeople that the Americans were going to move out and leave them to the Russians and the women would begin to plead and cry and offer us just about anything we wanted. Another of our pastimes was to smoke half of a cigarette, throw the rest on the ground and step on it, and then watch the civilians rush to pick it up as a prize. We could remember doing the same when we were on the other side of the gun. Once when I was working alongside the railroad tracks I had found a gold mine in the form of a pile of cigarette butts that had been dumped out of a train window while the train had been stopped there. Looking at it today, our behavior may look sadistic, but at the time, most of us felt at least a little justified in taunting German civilians.

. . . . .

In the morning I began to look for transportation westward. I was on my own and evidently free to do as I pleased, so I walked back to the highway and managed to hitchhike on a succession of American vehicles headed west. Along the way I came across several young German children who had obviously once been members of the Hitler Youth. They had cut off their long pants, removed the Hitler Youth insignia, adopted the postures of normal children and now made themselves hospitable to any Americans they encountered. It was interesting to see how quickly the German youth could adapt. I had also somehow acquired a can of sardines, which I prized greatly. I met an American GI who wanted it and was willing to trade a Hitler Youth knife for it. I made the trade, brought the knife home and gave it to my brother George.

Toward evening I found myself in a small German town and, along with several other American ex-POWs, found lodging in a school that the army was using for billeting stray liberated American prisoners. I became friendly with three other ex-POWs and the four of us decided to take a walk through the residential neighborhood. My companions this time were worldly

AMG Unit Hindenburg Kaserne

2 May 1945.

Pvt Frederick O. Scheer, ASN 14118781, is authorized to visit within curfew hours the City of PLAUEN and to re-enter the Hindenburg Kaserne.

types who clearly, as they say, knew the score. I was neither worldly nor did I know the score, but I went along for the ride. As we walked along the street, the three of them spotted what looked to them like an interesting house. They told me to wait outside and that they would be back in a few minutes. I did as they requested. In about half an hour, the three came out of the house with wide smiles on their faces. They never told me—nor did I ask—what had gone on inside that house, but in retrospect, I think I know.

The next morning I rose early and went back into town, where I discovered the headquarters of an American transportation unit. It was located near the center of town on the second floor of a two-story building that had been taken over for this purpose. I ambled up the stairway and over to a desk where a noncommissioned officer was seated. Just as I was about to report in and ask for transportation westward, a young German woman came into the office, went directly to the noncom's desk and began to wring her hands and speak frantically in German. She obviously spoke no English and the officer was totally baffled, not understanding a word she was saying. At that point I stepped up and volunteered my services, since by now I had a reasonable working knowledge of the German language—of pidgin German, anyway. It seems that the woman was trying to explain to the American authorities that she was seeking shelter and did not know which way to turn. The Americans had established separate housing arrangements for Jews and non-Jews, but she was half-Jewish and both facilities had denied her access. She was at a loss as to what to do. I meticulously translated the lady's dilemma to the American noncom, who, I assume, solved the problem, perhaps by sending her to the Red Cross. There were many situations like this one occurring all over the freed areas of Germany.

Once he had resolved the young woman's problem, the officer began to work on finding a solution to my situation. He provided me with transportation by GI truck to a nearby American airfield, where I met many other ex-POWs who were marshaling to be flown out of Germany. About 25 or 30 of us were herded toward a waiting Army Transport Command DC-3 aircraft. We climbed aboard the airplane and seated ourselves on the bucket seats, which had obviously once been used by paratroopers. This was the first time I had ever been in an airplane, but I was not apprehensive at all. I was just glad to be going home.

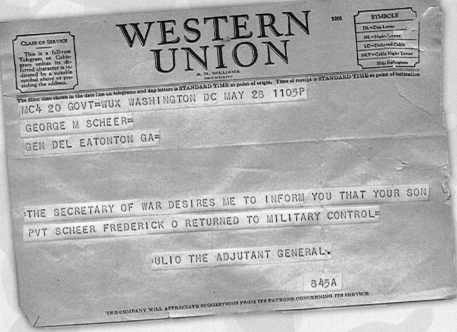

WESTERN UNION

1201

SYMBOLS

DL = Day Letter
NL = Night Letter
LC = Deferred Cable
NLT = Cable Night Letter
Ship Radiogram

CLASS OF SERVICE
This is a full-rate Telegram or Cablegram unless its deferred character is indicated by a suitable symbol above or preceding the address.

A. N. WILLIAMS
PRESIDENT

The filing time shown in the date line on telegrams and day letters is STANDARD TIME at point of origin. Time of receipt is STANDARD TIME at point of destination

MC4 20 GOVT=WUX WASHINGTON DC MAY 28 1105P

GEORGE M SCHEER=

GEN DEL EATONTON GA=

THE SECRETARY OF WAR DESIRES ME TO INFORM YOU THAT YOUR SON

PVT SCHEER FREDERICK O RETURNED TO MILITARY CONTROL=

ULIO THE ADJUTANT GENERAL.

845A

THE COMPANY WILL APPRECIATE SUGGESTIONS FROM ITS PATRONS CONCERNING ITS SERVICE

The flight to Le Havre on the Atlantic coast of France was relatively short. At the airfield in Le Havre, the occupants of this particular DC-3, and others that were arriving regularly, off-loaded onto GI trucks and were transported to nearby major marshaling centers. The American authorities had established these marshaling points in the area of Le Havre for returning prisoners-of-war. The centers were code named for American-made cigarettes. The particular camp to which I was assigned was called Lucky Strike. There were also camps named Marlboro and Camel. I was to be transported to Camp Lucky Strike, once again in an American GI truck. As we left the airfield at Le Havre and proceeded the short distance to Camp Lucky Strike, I saw that the countryside was an area of vast destruction. We passed several small towns, or at least the remnants of small towns, where nothing was standing: no buildings, no other structures, nothing but rubble. I wondered why the area had not been cleaned up; it had been almost a year since the Americans had stormed ashore in France. But it had not and all I saw was rubble. As we approached Camp Lucky Strike, driving slowly down a hillside from the north, I could see a vast plain toward the bottom of the hill. In that plain was a tremendous tent city with thousands and thousands of tents arranged in military order. Upon arrival each POW was given whatever sleeping materials he needed and assigned a particular cot in a particular tent, each of which housed anywhere from four to six GIs.

We reached Camp Lucky Strike on the 5th of May. The first thing I did after finding my bunk and settling in was to write a letter home. The letter reached Eatonton around May 10th and once again Mr. Nelson, seeing the name of the sender, ran all the way from the post office to my daddy's store to give it to him. Before long, the whole town knew I was free and safe.

Pvt. Frederick Scheer Freed in Germany

EATONTON, Ga., June 1. — A letter received this week by Mr. and Mrs. G. M. Scheer from their son, Private Frederick Scheer, 22, gave the family the first news that he had escaped from a German prison camp.

The letter, dated May 16, said he had escaped from the Nazis and crossed the American lines on May 1, and FREDRICK SCHEER that he expected to be home in a month.

His parents reside in Eatonton. George Scheer is a brother and Gloria and Frieda Scheer, sisters.

37 GEORGIANS LISTED AS FREED AT NAZI CAMPS

The War Department Thursday announced that three more Atlantians and 34 other Georgians have been freed from German prison camps.

They include:

EISENMAN, Arthur F., technical sergeant, husband of Mrs. Valeria E. Eisenman, Grady Hospital, Atlanta.

PETTIGREW, William B., second lieutenant, brother of Mrs. Stewart Clare, 631 Myrtle Street, Apt. 7, N. E., Atlanta.

THOMPSON, Norman L., technical sergeant, son of Mrs. R. L. Thompson, 830 St. Charles, Atlanta.

CALDWELL, Roger T., private first class, son of Mrs. Ida J. Caldwell, Route 1, Senoia.

CRATON, William I., technical sergeant, son of John H. Craton, Route 3, Dallas.

CURLES, Thomas C., private, son of Mrs. Lizzie M. Curles, Route 5, Moultrie.

DAVIS, Hubert M., staff sergeant, son of Mrs. Della B. Davis, 104 Pond Street, Toccoa.

DAVIS, William H., private first class, son of Mrs. Mattie B. Davis, 1317 Murphy Street, Augusta.

ESPY, Victory L., private first class, husband of Mrs. Dora H. Espy, general delivery, Trion.

FOUTS, Grady J., private first class, son of Sigal L. Fouts, Route 2, Douglasville.

GALLOWAY, Walter T., private first class, son of Mrs. Gertrude W. Galloway, Waynesboro.

GARRETT, Doya C., staff sergeant, son of William E. Garrett, 114 O Street, N. W. Thomaston.

GLISSON, Thomas W., corporal, son of Milton W. Glisson, Route 1, Claxton.

GLOVER, Cleveland, Sergeant, husband of Mrs. Edna L. Glover, 234 Sugar Refinery, Savannah.

GODBEE, James E., private first class, nephew of Mrs. Josie G. Boddiford, general delivery, Sylvania.

GOOD, Joseph R., Jr., private first class, husband of Mrs. Annabel R. Good, 1719 Walton Way, Augusta.

LOWERY, Thomas F., technician fifth grade, son of Eugene W. Lowery,

Route 2, Douglasville.

PALMER, John T., staff sergeant, son of John T. Palmer Sr., Box 106, Waynesboro.

PARRISH, Ruffies L., private, husband of Mrs. Hattie M. Parrish, Route 2, Stilson.

PERKINS, Enira C., private first class, son of Mrs. Jessie F. Perkins, Route 2, Chatsworth.

POWERS, Harold F., private, son of Mrs. Felton F. Powers, Route 3, Vienna.

PUTNAM, Grady W., sergeant, son of Mrs. Sarah Putnam, Route 11, Tunnel Hill.

SAVELL, Louis P., staff sergeant, brother of Mrs. Rosa L. Beasley, Route 2, Leary.

SCHEER, Frederick O., private, son of George M. Scheer, general delivery, Eatonton.

SMITH, Russell R., private, son of Mrs. Alma S. Smith, 243 Cave Spring Street, Rome.

SMITH, Stoy, private first class, son of Mrs. Allie Smith, 27 Scott Street, Commerce.

SMITH, Thomas P., staff sergeant, son of Mr. Bessie N. Smith, Route 2, McDonough.

STILL, Albert T., Sr., private, husband of Mrs. Kathleen L. Still, Route 1, Appling.

STRICKLAND, Charles M., private, husband of Mrs. Florris D. Strickland, Route 2, Box 398, Waycross.

SUTTON, Tommie C., private, son of Bunion C. Sutton, Route 2, Rochelle.

SUTTON, William H., sergeant, husband of Mrs. Dorothy S. Sutton, general delivery, Register.

TERRY, Harmon C., private, son of Mrs. Mary G. Terry, Suwanee.

TRULL, Joel L., private first class, husband of Mrs. Florence M. Trull, Route 2, Meigs.

WILLS, Homer B., first lieutenant, friend of Miss Marie Cannon, 109 N. Patterson Street, Valdosta.

WOMBLE, Johnnie L., staff sergeant, son of Walter E. Womble, Route 1, Cairo.

YORK, Charles R., staff sergeant, son of Mrs. Cleona W. York, Wayside Street, Cornelia.

YOUNG, Paul H., staff sergeant, son of Mrs. Mamie Gertrude Young, 11 Knoxville Street, Fort Valley.

A CARD OF THANKS—

We want to express to our friends our deep and humble gratitude for the many expressions of cheer and comfort conveyed us when the news of our son Frederick's escape from a German war prison camp was made known.

We want our friends to share in this happiness which has been twofold. The message of his liberation overwhelmed us- but hardly less has been the joy and deep humility at the wonderful response with which you have gladdened our hearts.

We could not have gone through the dark days but for faith in God's wisdom and the prayers of each of you.

Our joy is subdued in contemplation of the strength of soul and character of those whose messages were dread, all the more when we reveal that they sustained and cheered us in our hour of joy even though their hearts were weighted down with their own sorrow.

May we say again God bless each of you and thank you, thank you, thank you.

Mr. and Mrs. George M. Scheer and family.

Pvt. Frederick Scheer Escapes Prison Camp

On Tuesday of this week Mr. and Mrs. George Scheer received the following letter from their son, Pvt. Frederick Scheer, who had escaped from a German Prison Camp.

May 5, 1945

My Dearest Mother, Dad and All:

At last I will be coming home now. I don't know when I will see you but it will be about a month. I have quite a story to tell you when I return but that will keep. I hope Julian is somewhere close by. I think little Scheer will be thrilled when I tell him of our escape. I can hardly wait till I get back to the States. I hope I fly but I don't know yet. We came through the lines on May 1 and when I took the first G. I.'s hand and shook it I was so happy I could hardly stand up.

That's all for now. Hope home soon. Tell all ... oking for me...

CASUALTY BRANCH
THE ADJUTANT GENERAL'S OFFICE
Washington 25, D. C.

27 May 1945.

The accompanying 15-word message was filed in Europe for transmission by Army radiotelegraph facilities. However, due to the huge number of such messages filed by liberated American Military Personnel it became evident that faster delivery could be effected by sending the overload to the United States by air for mailing from Washington. The attached message was handled in this manner.

J. A. ULIO
Major General
The Adjutant General of the Army

1 Incl.

---

15 WORD FREE SENDER COMPOSITION PRIORITY MESSAGE

To: Mr. GEORGE SCHEER
(Full name of addressee)

(Street and number)

EATONTON GA.
(City or Town)   (State)

INSTRUCTIONS

One message only to next of kin in US from each Recovered American Military Personnel. PRINT message, including address and signature, in BLOCK LETTERS. Message, exclusive of address and signature, will be 15 words, one word above each of the 15 lines provided below.

DEAR	DAD	MOTHER	AM	IN
FRANCE	SHOULD	ARRIVE	AT	MAC
VERRY	SOON	LOVE	TO	ALL

FREDERICK SCHEER
(Full name of Sender)

14118781
(Army Serial Number)

DO NOT FOLD THIS FORM

This was my first letter to my folks after I escaped.

110

Camp Lucky Strike was close to a military landing strip that was used by American Air Force pilots to return aircraft from France and Germany to England and then to the United States. One of the things that all of us GIs remember vividly is that the American pilots—"hot pilots," as they were called—would buzz the camp before they landed their aircraft. Inevitably when this happened, we would all scramble to the floor and under the bunks, thinking that the war had commenced again and that we were being strafed one more time.

We were fed, clothed and treated with a great deal of respect at Camp Lucky Strike. In the late afternoons we would take our canteen cups, form long lines, much like the ones you see in amusement parks today, and file quietly by a dispensing point where eggnog, sans alcohol, would be poured into our cups. On one occasion a group of entertainers came and staged a revue similar to the Bob Hope shows filmed at military bases around the world that we would see years later. There were girls—beautiful girls, dancing girls—and male performers. It was during this show that I heard the song "Rum and Coca Cola" for the first time.

Anytime you have this many young men together in one place, there is bound to be a lot of complaining, griping and just plain bitching. Camp Lucky Strike was no exception. In spite of everything the American authorities did to make us comfortable, there were still many things that did not satisfy. Also, understandably, we were more than ready to go home. We realized that we were back with our own countrymen, out of the German prisons, but still we were anxious to be back with our loved ones in the United States. We dreamed of going home and finding it just the way we remembered it. Sometimes one of us would wake up in the wee hours of the morning to heed the call of nature and not be able to remember how to get to the bathroom in his own home, eventually realizing that he had been dreaming and was not at home just yet. Every day was another day of waiting, which was almost unbearable for us. As the days progressed, each day became more intolerable than the one before.

The griping grew in intensity to the point that the camp commander became aware of it and was somewhat upset by it. On the first Wednesday after I arrived, he called a general meeting of all the POWs in the camp. At his command we formed around the platform on which the USO performers had given their show. The commander stood on the platform and, aided by loudspeakers, emotionally addressed the thousands of assembled GIs. His message went something like this:

Look fellows, we know you want to go home and we are doing the very best we can. We, too, want you to go home. We will get you out just as soon as possible, but we simply cannot send everybody at once. You must be patient. We have to wait for the available transportation, which we are trying to marshal as quickly and as efficiently as we can. You must understand that the population of this camp, Camp Lucky Strike, has increased from 11,000 to 60,000 men since last Saturday—only four days ago.

This should give you a good idea of the number of Americans who had been captured and were being repatriated. Bear in mind that Camp Lucky Strike was only one of several camps processing American ex-POWs.

On May 8—between the time I wrote my letter home and the time it arrived—the Germans surrendered and the military interest began shifting from the European Theater of war to the Pacific Theater.

. . . . .

During the war there was also much movement of troops in the United States, sometimes even in Eatonton, Georgia. I enjoy telling one particular story about my mother and dad that is typical of their approach, not just to the war effort, but also to life in general.

One summer day in 1944, a troop convoy stopped in the middle of Eatonton. The men were permitted to disembark from the trucks for a lunch break, but they had no field kitchen, so they started looking around for a place to eat. They didn't have much of a choice because the only restaurant in Eatonton was the Uncle Remus Cafe, and it couldn't have held more than a few people.

My Daddy happened to look out the front of our store and saw a large group of soldiers milling around on the courthouse lawn. He went out to find out what was going on and asked one of the soldiers what was happening. When the soldier told him what the situation was, Daddy ran back into the store and called Mother at home. When she heard the story, she said, "George, you get Grover (the store's porter) and y'all go to both grocery stores and get all the bread, sandwich meat and mayonnaise they have and bring it here to the house." Mother, the cook and Grover made sandwiches and iced tea while Daddy went back to the courthouse and, pointing in the direction of our house, told all the soldiers he could find, "Y'all come on down to the house. We have sandwiches and iced tea for all of you. It's only two blocks that-a-way." My sister commented later that there were soldiers camped all over our big front porch and lawn that afternoon, eating sandwiches and drinking iced tea.

CHAPTER FOURTEEN
Home

The time at Camp Lucky Strike did come to an end about two weeks after I arrived. All of us were ultimately taken by truck to a nearby port—probably Le Havre—placed aboard American liberty ships and transported by sea back to the United States.

I was assigned to a ship with about 350 other American GIs. I remember affectionately the treatment that the others and I received on the voyage. Every one of us had his own bunk. We were served eggnog every night. We were treated as if we were something special, which, of course, we were.

When we arrived at the port of New York, we were transported from the docks to a marshaling center at the point of debarkation. It was there that I received my furlough home. I wasn't discharged from the Army—it took 60 points to get discharged and I had only 59—but I was given a 60-day pass to take leave at home until the processing-out procedure could begin.

It was morning when we reached the marshaling center, so the first thing we experienced there was breakfast. We were ushered into the huge mess hall where we picked up trays and eating utensils. As we moved down the serving line, German POWs dished out hotcakes and syrup. Things went smoothly until one of prisoners behind the serving counter switched off with another German and walked over to the spot in the serving line where the milk was iced down. He reached in; took out a quart of what must have been cool, delightful, sweet milk; walked to the back of the serving area and nonchalantly leaned back against the wall. There he popped the top of the milk bottle, tilted the bottle to his mouth and began to drink. One of the ex-POWs had just started to hold his tray up to receive his serving of hotcakes, but when he saw what the German was doing, he froze with his tray in midair, causing the server to dump the whole portion on the floor. The server screamed and cursed in German, whereupon the GI looked up at him with snarl and pointed at the German POW with the milk. This called the situation to the attention of the guys waiting in line and we nearly had a riot right there. For this group of American guys who had suffered so much under the control of the German Army, seeing this bastard of a German living the life of Riley was just too much for them to bear. Fortunately, the MPs removed

HEADQUARTERS RECEPTION STATION #15
Fort McPherson, Georgia

KPT/djh

SPECIAL ORDERS

23 JUN 45

NUMBER 1 7 4   E X T R A C T

6. Fol EM (W male) having rot US and rptd this Hq in compliance with
auth appearing below named reld fr atchd unasgd this sta and atchd unasgd in gr
to Redistribution Sta indicated for processing and reasgmt. Days TDY   and
tyl time indicated atnd. EM will rpt new sta on or before date indicated (all
dates 1945). In accordance AR 35-4820 FD will pay in advance prescribed monetary
alws in lieu rat for tyl a/r $1.00 per meal per man number meals indicated.
TCT PCS TDN FSA. 501-31 P 431-02 212/50425. Auth WD Ltr file AG 983.6 (6 Apr 45)
OB-S-A-SPGAN-M TAGO Washington 25 DC 21 Apr 45 Subj: Short Title: POW. EDCMR
26 Jun 45. R- 743 748

NAME	ASN	GRADE	BR.	MEALS	DAYS TYL	RPTG DATE	ADDRESS

AGSF MIAMI BEACH FLA   (LIBERATED POW) (PROJECT R) (ESCAPEES OR EVADEES)
Fol EM granted (60) days, (3) days tyl time, (7) meals, will rpt new sta on or
before 25 Aug 45.

*Henry, John C	6928002	Pvt	INF				Ellijay NC
*Phillips, Guy H	34916640	Pvt	INF				408 Church Jacksonville Ala
Marbry, Virgel L	34881334	Pvt	INF				Arlington, Tenn
Jackson, Dave	34900190	Pvt	INF				219 Ray Cooksville Tenn
Massey, Joseph A	34818876	Pvt	INF				Rt 1 Trussville Ala
McIntyre, Hugh D	34390717	Pvt	INF				220-47th Birmingham Ala
Mims, James C	34978055	Pvt	INF				Altoona Ala
Noe, Elmer J	34282072	Pvt	INF				401-4th Morristown Tenn
Oakes, Woodrow	34147221	Pvt	INF				Rt 1 Spencer Tenn
Smith, James E	34146289	Pvt	INF				1723-28th Nashville Tenn

Fol EM granted (61) days, (2) days tyl time, (5) meals, will rpt new sta on or
before 25th Aug 45.

*Kittle, William M	34766663	Pvt	INF				Ringgold Ga
*Buford, Oliver F	14041041	Pvt	INF				200 Anderson Marietta Ga
Tillery, Donald A	34442292	Pvt	INF				36 North Ave Rome Ga
Stephens, James C	34762453	Pvt	INF				RFD 1 Danielsville Ga
Scheer, Frederick O	14118731	Pvt	INF				Eatonton Ga
Newsome, J C	34910082	Pvt	CAV				609-9th Sanford Fla

Fol EM granted (63) days, (2) days tyl time, (5) meals, will rpt new sta on or
before 27 Aug 45.

Morgan, Laurin C	34689720	Pfc	INF				150 Sunset Athens Ga

Fol EM granted (64) days, (1) day tyl time, (3) meals, will rpt new sta on or
before 27 Aug 45.

Jordan, Harry L	34765981	Pfc	AAA				316 Parkway Atlanta Ga

(1st Ind ASF Hq Cp Patrick Henry Va 18 Jun 45 to Ltr Subj MO RO Gp E1036-15 A
Hq Normandy Base Sec Comm Z ETO 25 May 45)
*TPA (No extra tyl time atzd for TPA)
"Auth is granted to visit such additional places within the US as may be desired
during the period of this temporary duty for rehabilitation, recuperation and
recovery at no expense to the Government." (Auth WD TWX SPXOB-C 383.6 dtd 2 Jun
45)
EM named above last rat this sta to include noon meal and will lv 1400 23 Jun 45
by rail and/or bus. TR was not furn at this sta.

BY ORDER OF MAJOR DE WEES:

OFFICIAL:

KENNETH F. TAYLOR
1st Lt AUS
Asst. Adj.

JOHN L. BAKER
1st Lt AGD
Adj.

*This is a copy of the orders for my
60-day furlough at home.*

the German milk drinker and calmed down the people on both sides of the serving line. All went well after that.

I was given transportation by rail back to Atlanta. I had not told my folks when I would arrive; I figured I would just show up. Believe me when I tell you that I heard about that decision in a big way later. I spent the night in Atlanta with my uncle; my cousin Selma drove me down to Eatonton the next morning.

I remember very graphically the reunion with my mother and father, my two sisters and my brother at the old home place in Eatonton. One of Mother's little pleasures was to sit on the swing on the front porch and wait for the cook to come and fix breakfast. This is where she was when we drove up in front of the house. Dad had already made himself something to eat and had gone to the store. When Mother saw the car and then saw me getting out of it, she screamed, jumped up from the swing and ran down the porch steps to hug me and see that I was all there. After that emotional expression and physical inspection, she stepped back, put a serious frown on her face and asked "What time did you get into Atlanta and why didn't you call us?" When I admitted I had arrived the afternoon before, she almost had a fit. She soon calmed down, but I could still see some hurt in her eyes that I had seen other relatives first. I also remember with deep emotion and affection the glorious homecoming accorded me by the people of Putnam County. I was their lost and wandering son, now safely home.

During my 60-day furlough I again visited my cousin in Atlanta. While I was there, she introduced me to my wonderful wife, Gerry. We have been married over 60 years and have three grown children, two grandchildren and two great-grandchildren.

Mr. and Mrs. Frederick O. Scheer beginning their life together, 1947.

Afterword

In May of 2011, I was one of 64 WWII veterans invited to participate in an Honor Air Flight sponsored by the Roswell (Georgia) Rotary Club. We were escorted—each accompanied by a volunteer guardian—to Washington, D.C. where we visited the WWII, Korean War and Viet Nam memorials, and witnessed the changing of the guard at the Tomb of the Unkowns. The Honor Air program is a special project of the Roswell Rotary Club that was created to thank as many of us as possible for our service.

Alenda Kinder was my guardian on the Honor Air Flight to Washington.

Edwards Brothers Malloy
Ann Arbor MI. USA
June 29, 2017